D0456437

the war we can't lose

A devotional guide to
The Revelation

Henry Jacobsen

Published by
VICTOR BOOKS
A division of SP Publications, Inc.

Scripture quotations, unless otherwise noted, are from
The New American Standard Bible,
copyrighted by The Lockman Foundation. Used by permission.

Library of Congress Catalog Card No. 72-77013
ISBN: 0-88207-047-9
Printed in the United States of America

Contents

THREE INTERPRETATIONS OF THE REVELATION

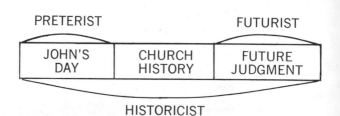

(This book accepts the Futurist view.)

THE SEALS, TRUMPETS, AND BOWLS

SEALS—1 2 3 4 5 6 7

TRUMPETS—1 2 3 4 5 6 7|
BOWLS—   1 2 3 4 5 6 7|

COMPARISON

TRUMPETS		BOWLS
1 HAIL, FIRE, BLOOD		SORES 1
2 ——————— SEA TO BLOOD ——————— 2		
3 ——————— RIVERS TO BLOOD ——————— 3		
		HEAT 4
4 ——————— DARKNESS ——————— 5		
5 LOCUSTS		
6 ——————— EUPHRATES ——————— 6		
7 ——————— EARTHQUAKE ——————— 7		

Not to
Tickle Itchy Ears

So many folks are interested in the future, today, that an abridged treatment of The Revelation should be of value as a sort of introduction to what the Bible has to say on this subject.

World conditions and international happenings suggest strongly that the history of mankind is rapidly approaching some sort of climax. Prophets of doom are expecting our civilization to go down the drain momentarily. Indefatigable optimists are sure man's scientific know-how is adequate to solve the problems that face him.

What is a Christian to think?

God, it happens, has a good deal to say about the future. He hasn't given us all the details, but He has made it clear, in the Bible, that by His sovereign will He is bringing His (not man's) purposes to pass. Men will neither usher in a golden age for themselves, nor will they destroy the planet. The future is in the capable hands of Almighty God.

This small volume, which you can read easily in much less than a day, deals with God's revelation of the future as found in the last book of the Bible. It will help you to study The Revelation as depicting the final conflict between God and Satan in the great warfare (cf. Eph. 6:10-18) that men have been involved in, whether they know it or not, since the time of Adam.

You will not find, in these pages, any fascinating speculations about the identity of Antichrist. No attempt is made to guess even the approximate date of the Rapture. There are no advance battle maps of World War III. It is not my purpose to tickle ears itchy for what God has not yet plainly revealed.

Instead, here is a short, terse, and hopefully lucid comment on the broad sweep of the book that tells us why God's people cannot lose this great war. I make no attempt to explain every symbol or interpret every verse. But this may be an advantage—you may get a better *overall* view of the book for not having been preoccupied with lesser details. And maybe this will whet your appetite for further study.

I have made a special effort to be "practical"—to draw from God's Word suggested applications of truth to life. This is in line with the purpose of the Holy Spirit in Scripture. Read Revelation 1:3 and 22:7!

By all means keep your Bible open and handy as you read. Never permit a book *about* Scripture to take the place of the Bible itself.

If the book is used in study groups—which I hope it will be—the person in charge would do well to use the *Leader's Guide* available for this purpose.

These chapters are an expanded version of the Bible study guides previously published in *Living Today*, supplemented with material prepared for the *Adult Teacher* by Dr. Merrill C. Tenney, who is generally recognized as an authority on this portion of the New Testament.

HENRY JACOBSEN

1

The War We Can't Lose

Revelation 1

Since the devil defeated Eve in the Garden of Eden, the earth has been the battleground of a titanic war between Good and Evil, between Right and Wrong, between God and Satan.

All mankind is involved in this conflict. Each individual is either fighting on God's side or on Satan's. No one is neutral, and in this war there are no conscientious objectors. And the casualties are staggering.

If you are an observant person, you have been aware of the conflict. Perhaps you have felt that Wrong seems to be winning the fight. Dishonesty, corruption, immorality, injustice, oppression, and godlessness are more prevalent today than ever before.

You may be tempted to suspect that Longfellow made a mistake when he wrote:

> The wrong shall fail,
> And right prevail,
> With peace on earth, good will to men.

But this war is unlike human wars, some of which drag on interminably and never come to a decisive conclusion. This war will end in a smashing victory for God and His forces.

No one can defeat the Lord God Almighty.

And the thrilling account of the great climax of the war between God and Satan, written in advance, is found in The Revelation.

As you read this book, don't be confused by the colorful, even flamboyant descriptions you find. Sometimes it is hard to distinguish between what is to be taken literally and what is symbolic. (Even scholars disagree, and only an excessively conceited person would insist that his interpretation *must* be right.)

As you read The Revelation, then, don't let preoccupation with the symbols and figures of speech bog you down. Don't miss the tremendous, majestic sweep of this stirring prophetic record of God's ultimate triumph.

As one would expect, The Revelation is Christ-centered. The Lord Jesus Christ came to this earth to redeem fallen man; He will come again to consummate the eternal purposes of God. It is He who will overthrow the forces of Satan and establish on earth His kingdom of righteousness and everlasting peace.

Some people, however, need to see Christ in a new perspective to understand how He will finally win the War of the Ages.

For example, does one get an adequate idea of Christ from these descriptive words and phrases?

Man of Sorrows
meek and lowly Jesus

Good Shepherd
Friend of sinners
Servant of Jehovah
the Nazarene
the Son of man

All these terms are commonly applied to our Lord. They are accurate, but they emphasize only one side of His nature. They do not give us an adequate concept of His sovereignty, power, and glory. They do not convey any impression of His holiness or His justice.

It is significant that the first chapter of The Revelation gives us another picture entirely of God's Son—a picture that emphasizes His omnipotence and His sovereignty. For The Revelation is our guarantee that one day our Lord will reign over earth—and that meantime He will meet your needs for protection, strength, wisdom, and self-realization.

Yes, the total adequacy of the Lord Jesus Christ, who one day will decide the destiny of nations, is available to you now, today. It can be a factor in your success as a husband, wife, or parent, in your effectiveness in home or at the office, and in whether you find life frustrating and disappointing or satisfying and adventurous.

Christ offers *you* poise, confidence, and peace of mind.

It's Understandable (Rev. 1:1-3)

The very name of The Revelation indicates that God gave it to us to *reveal* truth, not to *obscure* it. And the Lord promises a special blessing to a person who reads *and obeys* this part of Scripture (v. 3). Though The Revelation (sometimes miscalled "Revelations") is admittedly difficult, much of it is quite clear.

There are three principal views as to how one should interpret The Revelation:

1 It deals with conditions that existed at the time it was written, and describes these conditions in symbolic language.

2 It deals with the whole span of Church history from the first century to the return of Christ.

3 It deals with events that will take place just before the Lord returns to earth.

Though some evangelical scholars hold different views, this book accepts the third view as the correct one.

Keep in mind that God didn't give us The Revelation to entertain us, or to answer all our questions about the end of the age. The chief purpose of Scripture, almost always, is to influence our lives toward Christlikeness and to encourage us as we wait for and serve God's Son.

A Message for You (Rev. 1:4-11)

The Apostle John was the human author of The Revelation. When he was an old man he was banished, because of his Christian testimony, to Patmos, an island in the Aegean Sea, where he probably was put to forced labor in the mines. Under these unlikely circumstances he wrote this book, which describes a vision he had on Sunday ("the Lord's Day," Vincent).

John's Gospel, written earlier, puts emphasis on Christ's deity and His power over the circumstances and persons of men. It pictures Him as the Son of God.

The Revelation, last book of the New Testament to be written, continues the theme of the Gospel of John, but emphasizes the sovereignty of Christ over the forces of history. It reveals the manner in which He will set up His kingdom.

The correct title of the book is not "The Revelation of St. John the Divine," as some Bibles have it, but "The Revelation of Jesus Christ" (v. 1). Christ is the Source and Center of God's cosmic scheme for the redemption of individuals, of society, and of the universe (cf. Eph. 1:10). As you read The Revelation, open your heart to its presentation of Christ's glory and power and its picture of Him as King and Lord, and you will be stimulated to greater worship, devotion, and courage.

Christ is the faithful and true Witness (v. 5, AV). You may depend implicitly on His promises and trust your destiny confidently to Him. He is the Firstborn of the dead, and His resurrection authenticates His deity. He is Ruler of the kings of the earth—He will yet reign over the nations of the world. His coming in power is the great theme of The Revelation—and it is clear (cf. v. 7) that His return is to be no mere "spiritual" event, but a happening that will shake this earth to its very foundations.

Notice the simple summary of God's plan of redemption: He loved us, and this love prompted Him to release us from our sins by the blood of Christ, and to make us kings and priests (vv. 5, 6; 1 Peter 2:9).

"Alpha" and "Omega" (Rev. 1:8) are the "A" and the "Z" of the Greek alphabet. Jesus is the Beginning and the End. He was before Creation and He will survive all things. He is the Absolute—the one fixed point in a universe of flux and confusion—because He is God.

The Lord told John to send a record of this vision to the Christian churches located in seven cities of Asia Minor (v. 11), but since *all* Scripture is profitable for teaching and for instruction in righteousness, this book is worthy of the serious study of every Christian.

John was told (v. 19) to write three things:

1 "The things which you have seen"—that is, a description of his vision of the risen Lord (vv. 10-18).

2 "The things which are"—that is, a description of conditions in the time in which He was living.

3 "The things which shall take place after these things"—that is, a prophecy of future events.

"Futurist" interpreters (the view presented in this book) of The Revelation take these three points as an outline of the book, viz.,

The vision John saw (chap. 1)

Conditions in the churches of his time (chaps. 2 and 3)

Events which would take place in the future (chaps. 4—22).

Our Risen Lord (Rev. 1:12-30)

You will hardly need to be told that verses 13-16 are not a literal, photographic description of the glorified Christ in heaven.

Suppose a savage from the heart of Africa were to visit this country and try to write his friends, in his own language (assuming he were literate), about electric lighting, television, self-operating elevators, and computers. He would find his experience and his vocabulary woefully inadequate.

John was in a somewhat similar position. He was inspired to write about something entirely foreign to human experience. The Holy Spirit gave him the words to use, but human language simply is not equal to the task of dealing with heavenly realities. Much as Ezekiel does in his vision of the glory of God (Ez. 1), Revelation gives an *impression* of the Lord's appearance rather a literal description.

When symbolic language is taken literally, it becomes grotesque. Christ does not *literally* walk around in heaven among seven lampstands. He does not *literally* carry a sword in His mouth.

John's first readers, knowing the Old Testament, would understand that the Lord's long, flowing robe and golden belt were symbols of royalty. His flaming eyes indicated He can see into men's hearts. The sword spoke of the incisiveness of His Word (cf. Heb. 4:12, 13). His glory was represented by the way His face was like the shining sun. The seven golden lampstands represented the seven churches of Asia Minor to which John was to write (Rev. 1:20). The seven stars John saw were the "angels," or messengers, of the seven churches.

The lampstands were separate. Each church has a testimony to bear in its own place. And the glorified Lord was walking among the lampstands. He is watching and testing His churches as they fulfill their function—to give light to the world (cf. Matt. 5:14).

No wonder John fell at the Lord's feet! If Christians today had an adequate idea of Christ's power and glory, they would do likewise.

The risen Lord's word to John is His word to you: "Do not be afraid!" (v. 17)

This is Christ's message for His people in every age. Regardless of the uncertain world in which you live, regardless of the problems you face, He reassures you with His "Don't be afraid!"

Our Lord is on the throne and His purposes for you are sure. You are safe in Him. This does not mean you will not be tested, or that you will be spared illness, financial difficulties, and the other "tribulations" that are man's lot on earth. It *does* mean that God will give you what it takes to undergo life's trials "not somehow, but triumphantly."

Your confidence, however, is to be based entirely on God. Man's efforts at world-betterment and self-improvement have their place, but they will never bring about God's purposes.

But because God is sovereign, His purpose cannot fail. The war between Good and Evil, between God and Satan, is the war you *cannot* lose—if you are on God's side.

2

Cooling Off

Revelation 2:1-17

Ted and Sally Brown are in their early 30s and have three children. They have a comfortable home and Ted is the successful operator of a service station. He and Sally have been loyal church members ever since they became Christians in their teens.

In recent months, though, they have not been attending church services regularly.

"We just seem to have lost the desire to go to church," Ted explains to Pastor Swanson, who is calling on them and has mentioned that they have been missed.

"To be honest," Ted concludes, "we've sort of slipped up on family devotions and Bible reading, too. It's not that we don't believe, or that we're busier than usual. It's just . . . well, I guess maybe we've just cooled off spiritually, or something."

It isn't unusual for a Christian's zeal to cool now and then—sometimes to the extent that he loses almost all interest in God, the Bible, and church-related activities.

People in this condition are sometimes called

backsliders. Whatever they are called, it's bad news.

And a whole church can cool off, too.

Our Scripture tells us about an early church that cooled, losing its warm, spontaneous love for the Lord Jesus. The consequences of this sort of cooling, whether in an individual or in a local church, are always disastrous—unless the condition is corrected.

Some Bible scholars think each of the seven churches in Asia Minor to which John sent the message given him by the glorified Lord, represents a definite period in Church History. Ephesus, they think, portrays the Church during the Apostolic Period. Smyrna represents the Church under intense persecution by the state, as in the time of the Roman Emperor Nero. Pergamos represents the Church in Constantine's day, enjoying the imperial favor of the Roman government—and the special temptations that go with such a position.

Orthodox but Unloving (Rev. 2:1-7)

The church at Ephesus was typical of many orthodox churches today. It was sound in doctrine, energetic in defending the faith, and patient in enduring persecution. It diligently fought false teaching.

God sees your acts of kindness, patience, and loyalty even when others fail to notice them. He did not overlook the virtues of the Ephesian church. But He had something against this assembly of believers—just as He has a complaint, today, against many believers (or churches) whose doctrinal beliefs are completely "sound."

The Lord found the Ephesians lacking in love for

Him, and He found them lacking love for one another.

Their devotion had cooled off.

How about *your* love and devotion? Are *you* in the condition of Ted and Sally Brown? Are you hiding your loss of love by "going through the motions" of attending church, holding family devotions, and telling no one how empty and superficial your "religious" practices are?

Is Bible reading a chore, church-going intolerable, and prayer almost impossible? Is God *unreal* to you?

Here's good news!

God doesn't surrender a church or an individual without a struggle! In Old Testament days Jehovah was reluctant to hand His nation Israel over to punishment (Hos. 11:8). And Christ, in John's vision, wanted to salvage the Ephesian church—not to destroy it.

The Lord remembered how hard the Ephesians had worked for him (Rev. 2:2). They had witnessed to a pagan population. Their illiterate hearers were probably dull and unresponsive; their educated hearers were doubtless scornful and sarcastic. Witnessing was hard work!

Prayer is labor, preaching is labor, and visitation was labor in a day when one traveled on foot. It's still labor even when a car is available.

The Ephesians had showed patience by their willingness to stay together even when they were few in number. When a new church does not grow rapidly and its future seems uncertain, it is easy to succumb to the temptation to go to another church that appears to be more prosperous.

In Ephesus there was no flagrant immorality, no denial of the truth, no slacking of activity, no tolerance of evil. The sin of Ephesus was *complacency*.

This is the ailment that so often attacks orthodox Christians. Confident of their doctrinal correctness, they often rest on their orthodoxy and fail to show others the love God wants them to reflect. They ignore such Bible teachings as: "The one who does not love does not know God, for God is love" (1 John 4:8).

The final outcome of the Ephesians' loss of love was that their lampstand was taken away from them. They lost their opportunity to be lights in the world's darkness. A heart cold toward God soon becomes cool toward others. Doctrinal correctness with an unloving heart never results in effective testimony. And it is tragic that people who accuse Christians of being unloving are so often right.

The Lord told the Ephesians to do three things: remember, repent, and repeat (Rev. 2:5).

As a motorist drives eastward from the foothills of the Rocky Mountains, he may not realize, because the descent is gradual, how fast he is losing altitude. When he is finally aware of the warmer air of the plains and looks back, he sees the hills behind him and knows how far down he has come.

The first thing necessary if you are to get back your original power—or love—is for you to recognize how much of it you have lost. You will be helped, in doing this, by recalling the love that probably filled your heart when you first came to Christ.

The second part of the remedy is to repent, which means to change your mind. This involves not merely revising your opinion on one or two points, but adopting God's whole point of view, as it is revealed in Scripture, toward sin and holiness. It includes forsaking your sins and returning to the standards God gives to His people in His Word.

The third part of Jesus' remedy is summarized in the word "repeat"—to "do the deeds you did at first" (v. 5).

The Ephesians were still active, but their deeds had come to lack the loving concern that had originally prompted them. Their work had lost its faith, their labor was without love, and their patience was without hope (cf. 1 Thes. 1:3). In other words, the Ephesian church was settling into a rut. And a rut has been likened to a grave with the end knocked out.

These three steps—remember, repent, and repeat —are still the route back to a love relationship with God, with fellow Christians, and with other men.

Each of the letters to the seven churches ends with a promise of reward for those who overcome in spite of their hard or dangerous circumstances (cf. vv. 7, 11, 17). We can't fully understand the nature of all these rewards, but you may be certain that they are tremendously worthwhile.

"Rich"—or Really Rich? (Rev. 2:8-11)

Smyrna, the city in which the second of the seven churches was located, was one of the wealthiest towns in Asia Minor. In the eyes of its affluent citizens, the believers there were poverty-stricken. But in the sight of God the Smyrnan Christians, whose treasure was laid up in heaven, were rich.

Men tend to think of wealth in terms of the material things—including money—that a person owns. They forget that *things*, however pleasant it is to own them, are here today and gone forever tomorrow.

A well-known manufacturer of fine clothing has for his slogan, "Our best advertisements are not written—they are worn." The testimony of Smyrna was so apparent to all who knew these Christians that it was not necessary for the Lord to "advertise" it. This church is the only one of the seven for which the Lord has no criticism.

God makes it plain, however, that more suffering was ahead for the Christians at Smyrna. They were being persecuted by the Jews. The synagogue, which had once served as a springboard for the preaching of the Gospel, was fast becoming the bitter enemy of the new Church.

The believers at Smyrna were not to be afraid of suffering. It would last only "ten days"—a limited length of time. Christians of every age are called to endure suffering, but they need not fear it. It is always under God's control.

Tolerating Immorality (Rev. 2:12-17)

Pergamos, site of the church to which the third letter was addressed, was a city of political and religious prominence. It was full of magnificent shrines, some of which were dedicated to Greek gods and others to emperor worship. Here Christians met both political and religious opposition, but God knew all about the problems of living in the place where Satan had made his home (v. 13) and was able to defend His people.

No matter how virulent the devil's attacks may be, God will see you through if you are depending on Him.

The Lord rebuked the Pergamos Christians because they were tolerating false teachers in their midst. Loss of one's first love for God and His Word often leads to general backsliding, and this includes lack of spiritual discernment and inability to distinguish what is true from what is false.

These traits are all too common in the professing Christian church today. Lack of discernment accounts for the fact that many men are preaching, from "Christian" pulpits, a message that has nothing to do with God's truth.

The Christians at Pergamos, for instance, accepted the teachings of the Nicolaitans and of Balaam. We aren't too sure exactly what the Nicolaitans taught, but Balaam was the mercenary prophet whom Balek hired to curse Israel (Num. 22–25). When God would not allow Balaam to carry out Balek's order, the prophet showed Balek how to defeat the Hebrews by leading them into idolatry and sexual uncleanness. False doctrine seems, as often as not, to be accompanied by immorality.

The devil attacked the Ephesians by causing them to let their affection for Christ grow cool. He tried to corrupt the Smyrnans through suffering. In Pergamos, he seduced Christians by getting them to assimilate heathen practices into the church. Corruption is often the price the Church pays when it enjoys the favor of the government.

At times the Church, like some individuals, thrives best in hardship. Sometimes it cannot seem to stand easy, prosperous times.

In any case, God doesn't overlook the faults of His Church—and He won't overlook your faults. He judges impartially, whether He is dealing with a church or with an individual. He knows your every sin—but He doesn't reject you. Rather, He calls you to repentance and encourages you by His promises of forgiveness and reward. He challenges you to overcome in the strength He wants to give you.

The seven messages of Revelation 2 and 3 were sent to the churches as corporate bodies, but notice that the final appeal is always to each individual church member—"to *him* that overcometh" is the call, not "to *them* that overcome." The Lord says, "*He* who has an ear"—the *individual* who is ready to respond to the call of God—"let *him* hear what the Spirit says."

The Holy Spirit is calling you to an orthodoxy kindled by love, to a faithfulness that is not afraid of suffering, and to a persistence in Christian character that will find no place for compromise with false teaching or sin.

3

Opportunity Unlimited

Revelation 2:18—3:22

Jim Burke and John Jones attend the same church and are junior executives in the same company. Both men take Christianity seriously and are concerned over their responsibility to tell others about the Lord. Both have warm personalities and a friendly way of speaking.

Whenever Jim travels on a bus, train, or plane, he finds some pretext for talking to the person next to him about the Lord. In fact, sometimes he doesn't even wait for an opportunity. He *makes* one! He's really eager to share his faith.

John, on the other hand, is more reticent. If someone talks to him about religion, the Church, the state of morals, or the international prospects, he will probably "witness," but not otherwise.

"I wait for an open door," John says—but he admits the door doesn't open very often.

"I push the door open," laughs Jim.

The remainder of Revelation 2 and 3 contains letters to the other four churches of Asia Minor. Included is the church at Philadelphia, to which the risen Christ opened a door to service, and the church at Laodicea, which had cooled off even more than Ephesus.

Let's think especially about the Philadelphian church.

Slipping, Standing, Moving (Rev. 2:18-29)

To the church at Thyatira, Christ appeared in awesome majesty. His eyes were like a flame of fire and His feet were like brass. The description suggests His omniscience and His authority to judge.

The Christians at Thyatira were known for their love, zeal, faith, and patience. Their church had not deteriorated as had the one in Ephesus. Too often, a great initial momentum falls off—either in a church or in an individual. Are you slipping back, standing still, or making progress in your spiritual growth and your Christian service?

The Lord Jesus rebuked the Thyatira church for harboring an evil woman who claimed to be a prophetess. Though she posed as a religious leader, she led many astray. It is not certain whether the fornication she tried to combine with Christian doctrine and practice was physical or spiritual. In either case, she was weaning hearts away from God. In any age, men commit idolatry when they allow anything or anyone to usurp God's first place in their lives.

God had given this evil prophetess opportunity to repent, but she had refused. Now she was to be judged, and her children (v. 23) would share her doom. What sort of influence have you on *your* children? Parenthood has great privileges—and great responsibilities. To misuse them is very serious.

The Lord praised the church at Thyatira for her zeal (v. 19)—her love, faith, patience, and service. It would seem, from these words, that in some ways Thyatira was an *effective* church.

Living—but Dead (Rev. 3:1-6)

When John wrote The Revelation, Sardis was a city of the past. It had ceased to be important.

The church at Sardis had a reputation for vitality, but it was really in a condition almost as bad as that of the city itself. It was inwardly dying.

It is easy for a church—or an individual believer —to keep up an outward appearance.

A church may engage in a lot of organizational activities, be well attended, and have a wonderful reputation—and be spiritually dying or dead.

A Christian may attend services and hold offices, teach a Sunday School class, conduct family devotions, and still know, in his heart, that there is no reality, no vitality, in all he does.

It is a dreadful thing to have a name for being a Christian and to know that one is merely putting on an act.

Christ urges us (vv. 2, 3) to recognize our true condition and to repent before the time available to us runs out. If we don't, we may even be surprised by the Lord's coming.

Our Lord knows the condition of every person in a church. He knows the few who have not defiled their garments by false doctrine or by immorality. You pay a fearful price if you compromise with doctrinal error or indulge in impure thinking or actions. And the "new morality," which has overcome so many persons today, is only the old immorality in disguise.

Old-fashioned morals (cf. v. 4) may not make you popular, but the disapproval of the majority is of no importance to one whose name is written in the Lamb's book of life.

Feeble—but Faithful (Rev. 3:7-13)

Ancient Philadelphia was a center of Greek culture, situated on an important trade route. The church located here was superior to others in several ways. It was not strong, but was loyal to the Lord and true to His Word. It was bitterly opposed by the Jews of the city, who prided themselves on being God's chosen people. Actually, they were tools of Satan (v. 9). They remind us of people today who boldly oppose God's work and God's people in the name of religion. A number of sects and cults—and, to an increasing degree, such evils as witchcraft, demonology, and satanism—would come under this condemnation.

Pious persecutors of the true Church will one day receive the due penalty for their evil. They will recognize that they have persecuted God's own people. The Lord promises Christians that He is coming quickly (v. 11), and urges them to hold on to what they have, that no one take their crown.

He also promises that He will provide special protection for them during the period of testing that is to come on earth (v. 10). Some see in this verse the promise that the Rapture of the Church will occur before the Great Tribulation begins. Certainly this promise challenges believers to loyalty and trust.

You have no doubt learned, perhaps from personal experience, that God does not always protect His people from danger and hardship. Christians have automobile accidents, are victims of evil men, and suffer sickness and disability much as unbelievers do. The difference is that God is with His people in their trials (Isa. 43:1, 2), and that all things work together for a believer's ultimate good (Rom. 8:28, 29).

The Lord found no real fault with the church at Philadelphia. He pointed out merely that it was weak (v. 8). It had only "a little power." Nevertheless, it had kept His Word and had not denied the faith.

Christ is seen, in this letter, as the God of holiness, truth, and authority, who overcomes all opposition. He carries the key of David, a symbol of power and authority. He opens doors and no man can shut them; He shuts them and no man can open (v. 7).

The Lord gave the Philadelphian church "an open door"—that is, an unlimited opportunity for service. And He is still opening the door, or preparing the way, for His people to help others, to tell them about His love, and to invite them to put their trust in the Saviour.

Unfortunately, some Christians don't recognize an open door when they see it. They keep asking God to use them, when all the while they have opportunities to befriend needy or lonely neighbors, to do visitation work for their local church, or to encourage their Sunday School teachers and their pastors. They are confronted by numberless opportunities to invest their means in God's work. Missionaries and others need their prayer support.

The doors stand wide open!

Other believers do not realize that the door is shut. They waste time, effort, or money trying to do something that is not in God's purpose for them. They are teaching when they should be taking care of nursery children, or singing in the choir when they should be visiting. Or they are working at something long before the proper time comes—or long after it has passed.

It takes spiritual discernment to recognize the exact time when God wants us to go ahead.

God promised overcomers in Philadelphia that He would make them pillars in His temple. Pillars symbolize solidarity and permanence—highly desirable qualities in a city which, like Philadelphia, was known for many earthquakes. These pillars also symbolize relationship, for the name of God was to be inscribed on them.

Some scholars believe the church at Philadelphia represents the true Church in our own time—feeble in relation to the wicked world around her, but loyal to God and His truth. These interpreters see in the last church, Laodicea, the *professing* church of today.

Satisfied—but Lukewarm (Rev. 3:14-22)

Laodicea, last of the seven cities of Asia Minor named in these chapters, was the home of a rich, self-satisfied church. The budget was oversubscribed year after year, the secretary wrote glowing reports of the business meetings, and members enjoyed their pot-luck suppers in fellowship hall. So far as they were concerned, their church was a great success.

But the Lord rebuked the Laodicean church for its lack of every desirable quality. There may have been a great deal of social life and business activity, but spiritually the church was insipidly lukewarm. God would reject her.

The Laodiceans thought of themselves as rich and well off, but God said they were wretched, miserable, poor, blind, and naked.

This church is a picture of a person who is satisfied with a religion that is merely "a form of godliness," and who fancies that going through certain rites and ceremonies, and holding membership in the "right" denomination, and believing a prescribed doctrinal statement, will take the place of genuine purity, holiness, and godliness.

This mistake is not limited to people who belong to "liberal" churches. It is perfectly possible to believe all the right doctrines and yet be spiritually lukewarm.

The church at Ephesus had lost her first love; she had started to cool off. The church at Laodicea had cooled off to the extent that she was now quite tepid, or lukewarm. And this condition is an abomination in God's sight. He will not stand for it. "Because you are lukewarm, and neither cold nor hot," He warns, "I will spit you out of My mouth" (v. 16).

The only remedy for such an individual or church is to acquire true riches (spiritual wealth), clean raiment (the righteousness that God credits to those who trust in Christ), and healing eyesalve (spiritual discernment). God is able and willing to supply these qualities (v. 18) to those who come to Him through personal trust in His Son. He will make you rich with the true riches; He will cover your spiritual nakedness; he will open the eyes of your soul so that you may see yourself as you are and recognize the redeeming truth of His Word as it is in Jesus Christ.

There is tenderness in the Lord's message to this backslidden, apostate church. He speaks of Himself as standing at the door knocking, waiting to be admitted, longing to enjoy intimate fellowship.

He stands at the door of your heart also. The latch to that door, as Holman Hunt pictured it in his famous painting, is on the inside. The Lord can enter only as you allow Him to. You do this by admitting your helplessness to save yourself and your willingness to receive Him as your Saviour.

Though it is the Lord who opens the door of opportunity for His people, He will never force His way in at the door of your heart. He waits for you to give Him opportunity to enter.

If you are not a Christian, why not open the door today for Christ to become your Saviour?

And if you *are* a Christian, why not walk through whatever door He has opened to you to serve Him?

The opportunities for service to God were never greater!

4

Something to Sing About

Revelation 4 and 5

Don Wainright is a fine person—a fellow it is easy to be with. He is the life of a party, he and his wife are always doing things for people, and Mrs. W. is at every service of their church. So is Don—until the golfing season begins. Then he takes off from his splitlevel early Sunday morning and returns only after he has played from 18 to 36 holes.

"God made the out-of-doors," he glows, "and I love to fellowship with Him there. I worship best under the blue sky that reminds me of the Creator. Fresh air is much more conducive to true worship than stained-glass windows and organ music!"

A good many Christians have fuzzy ideas about the nature, basis, and purpose of worship.

Some confuse worship with prayer. We can—and often do—worship God in prayer, but prayer in itself is not worship.

Strictly speaking, worship is the adoration of God —that is, expressing our awareness of His majesty, goodness, love, power, and other attributes.

When a person steps into the nave of a mighty cathedral, the lofty arches, the pealing organ music, and the filtering of sunlight through the stained glass windows are likely to affect him. What he feels, however, is not necessarily worship—it may be an *emotional* reaction. Worship involves emotion, to be sure, but it is primarily a *spiritual* exercise.

If you depend on atmosphere to create a "mood" of worship, it is possible that what you call "worship" is merely a natural response to beauty—or just a pleasant, relaxed sensation perhaps brought on by soft organ music.

True worship grows out of one's relationship with God, not out of one's surroundings. Some environments are more conducive to worship than others, but one *can* worship God acceptably under *any* circumstances.

One *can* worship God on the golf links, or walking through the countryside, or fishing on a lake. Usually, however, one doesn't—even if one is a Christian.

Invited to "Come up" (Rev. 4:1, 2a)

After John was given the letters for the seven churches of Asia Minor, he noticed that a door to heaven had been opened, and heard himself invited to "come up hither" to be shown "what must take place after these things" (v. 1).

This phrase introduces the third major division of the book. From this point, the remainder deals with events that in John's day were still future. According to most interpreters, these events are still future today.

Worship at the Throne (Rev. 4:2b-11)

John doesn't give us a complete description of heaven, by any means, but he had a glorious vision of the majestic throne of God. God's throne—which symbolizes His sovereignty—is the central feature of heaven and of the universe, the point of reference from which everything in heaven is located—"about the throne," "out of the throne," "before the throne," "in the midst of the throne."

God the Father, who sat on the throne, is a Spirit, and John does not try to describe Him. He did, however, see God's glory, which took the form of rays of light such as would be reflected by precious stones.

Round the throne John saw a rainbow, a symbol of God's mercy (Gen. 9:12-15). Lightnings and thunderings suggested God's majesty. The lamps John saw represented the Holy Spirit, the Illuminator.

Each person of the Trinity is mentioned in this passage.

Around the throne were four living creatures (called "beasts" in the AV). Their many eyes symbolize penetrative knowledge. They may be the cherubim or the seraphim (Ez. 1:4-6, 10), who guard the holiness of the throne, and some believe that the description of them in Revelation 4:7 indicates that they symbolize the entire animate creation—all living things.

In a circle around the throne were 24 seats, or thrones, on which sat 24 elders. They represented the 12 tribes of Israel and the 12 apostles of the Early Church. They joined in the song of redemption sung in heaven, which may suggest that they represent all the redeemed men and women of both Old Testament and New Testament times.

The worship of heaven was led by the living creatures and was taken up by the 24 elders. The creatures praised God because of His eternal nature (vv. 8, 9). The elders praised Him because of His worthiness as Creator and Sovereign (vv. 10, 11).

The worship of heaven is unceasing—"day and night" (v. 8). Such a prospect is unattractive to many people. We sing about "the pure delight of a single hour" that we spend in prayer, but most of us would really prefer an extra hour of sleep.

God's Unfolding Purpose (Rev. 5:1-7)

John noticed that the One on the throne was holding a scroll (lit.) sealed with seven seals. The fact that the scroll was sealed indicates that it was some sort of official document, and that not everyone had a right to break the seals. Apparently the seals were arranged in such a way that each time a seal was broken it exposed part of the scroll to view.

Some think that the scroll represents the title deed to the universe, which man forfeited when he sinned. From chapter 6, however, it is more reasonable to conclude that the scroll contained the purposes of God for the world.

An angel appeared and asked for a volunteer to break the seals and unroll the scroll (v. 2). To do this was a symbolic action equivalent to unfolding, or revealing, or even bringing to pass, the purpose of Almighty God.

In response to the angel's challenge, no one appeared. No one on earth, in heaven, or under the earth was qualified for this great privilege. The taint of sin ruled out all men, and in heaven there was no one who could fairly represent the human race.

John wept at the thought that the scroll might not be opened. Perhaps he was afraid that God's purposes for earth would never come to pass, and that the world would never be cleansed of the power and defilement of sin.

Maybe you, too, have felt discouraged and distressed because of the seemingly overwhelming strength of sin and evil in today's social order.

But John stopped his tears when he heard the announcement that "the Lion of the tribe of Judah" was worthy to open the scroll. This name cannot possibly apply to anyone other than the Lord Jesus Christ. But as John looked for a lion to appear, he saw, in the midst of the throne, "a little lamb" (v. 6, lit.).

Don't let John's description of the Lamb distress you. Its throat had been cut (lit.) and it had seven horns and seven eyes. The description is not photographic, or literal. This is symbolic language used to convey spiritual truth. The eyes represent Christ's omniscience, and the Lamb is a symbol of Christ as God's great Sacrifice for sin (cf. John 1:29). The marks of the Lamb's death suggest Calvary.

The Revelation portrays Christ as sovereign Lord, who will at last exercise His right to reign on earth. It also pictures Him as the Lamb of God, who died for your sin. Have you acknowledged Him as such? Before He can be your Lord and Master, He must be your Saviour.

Many persons admire Jesus as a man. They admit that He was the flower of humanity, a paragon of virtue, the best Teacher who ever lived. The only people who will worship Him in heaven, however, are those who will praise and extol Him as "the Lamb of God, who takes away the sin of the world" (John 1:29).

The worship of heaven, then, is closely linked with the salvation God makes available through His Son. It is by virtue of His worthiness in having prevailed over the powers of sin that the Lamb was able to take the scroll from the One who sat on the throne. Our Lord is eminently worthy to reveal and to bring to pass the final purposes of God.

"Me a Priest?" (Rev. 5:8-14)

The Lamb's taking the scroll marked a great climactic moment in heaven. It was the signal for the four living creatures and the 24 elders to prostrate themselves in worship before the throne. And this time their worship was directed toward God the Son. They adored Him as "worthy" because He had redeemed them by His precious blood.

Bible scholars differ as to just *when* the Lamb takes the scroll.

Some think that this event happened when the risen Christ returned to heaven 40 days after He had left the grave. They believe the rest of The Revelation is a symbolic summary of the course of history since Pentecost.

A more likely view held by others is that the scene described in chapters 4 and 5 will occur after the Rapture of the Church (which they link with "Come up here," 4:1) and as the Great Tribulation gets under way on earth. According to this view, the remainder of the book concerns future events.

It is important to note that no race, no nation, no denominational group has a monopoly on the love of God. His grace goes out to "every tribe and tongue and people and nation" (v. 9).

How about *your* love and concern? Is it limited to your family, your local church, or your nation? Adopt a broader perspective!

God's purpose in redemption is to make His people priests (v. 10). It is your privilege and your duty to speak to men for God and to pray to God for men.

Then John heard a great chorus of angels join the living creatures and the elders in another anthem (v. 11). This song didn't mention redemption, for the unfallen angels hadn't sinned and didn't need to be redeemed.

As John listened, he heard the triumphant song taken up not only in heaven but throughout all the universe. "Every created thing which is in heaven and on the earth and under the earth and on the sea, and all things in them, I heard saying, "To Him who sits on the throne, and to the Lamb, be blessing and honor and glory and dominion forever and ever."

Our Lord is worthy of the worship of heaven.

He is also worthy of your trust, your worship, and your glad service.

Does He have them?

5

They Are Riding Now

Revelation 6:1—8:5

You have often heard, of course, of the Four Horsemen of the Apocalypse (which is another name for the book of The Revelation).

Just for the fun of it, why not take a small test at this point? Before you read on, check those of the following that are among the horsemen described in Revelation 6. (If you want to take an advanced test, indicate by each term you check whether that horseman is first, second, third, or last of the four:

Death	*Imperialism or Conquest*
Depression	*War*
Communism	*Juvenile Delinquency*
Immorality	*Economic Distress*
Pestilence	*Famine*

If you don't do too well on this test, you are an average Christian. In view of the promise of blessing for those who read and obey The Revelation, few believers know The Revelation as well as they ought to.

Let's review briefly the first five chapters of the book:

Chapter 1 tells us of John's vision of the ascended, glorified Lord Jesus Christ.

Chapters 2 and 3 contain the Lord's messages to the seven churches of Asia Minor.

Chapters 4 and 5 describe the glorious worship of God the Father and of His Son, our Redeemer, around the throne in heaven.

With chapter 6 we get into the stirring prophecy of coming judgment.

Not all of us will be on earth when these cataclysmic events take place, but *every* unbeliever without exception must one day stand before the Judge of all the earth. Only Christians, whose sins have been forgiven because of personal trust in Jesus Christ, will avoid the blasting torrent of divine wrath.

Trouble after Trouble (Rev. 6)

The Lord Jesus Christ, the Lamb who had been slain, was qualified by His work of redemption to open the seven seals on the scroll that He had taken from His Father's hand.

As He broke the seals, the progressive steps in God's work of judging sin and establishing order on earth were revealed. These events, described in chapters 6 and 7, are closely related to Christ's return.

• *Conquest* (Rev. 6:1, 2). When the Lamb broke the first seal, one of the four living creatures commanded, "Come!" and John saw a white horse appear. Its rider wore a crown, carried a bow, and went forth to conquer.

This rider has been variously identified as Christ

or as Antichrist, but he undoubtedly represents the spirit of imperialism, or military conquest. This spirit has plagued mankind since earliest times. One after another, great empires have taken shape, conquered, and been conquered. The have-nots have always schemed against the haves, and the haves are always trying to exploit the have-nots. The spirit of conquest, like the poor, is always with us.

• *War* (vv. 3, 4). The second horseman was obviously war, which follows inevitably when the spirit of conquest dominates a situation. The League of Nations and the United Nations have not succeeded—nor will they succeed—in eliminating war.

There have always been "wars and rumors of wars," but they have become more and more frequent and more and more intensive. Today the threat of global holocaust hangs heavily over the entire earth.

The second rider rode a red horse, the color doubtless representing the oceans of blood that have been shed in the wars of all ages.

• *Famine* (vv. 5, 6). The third horseman rode a black horse, symbol of drought and famine. He suggests scarcity of staple foods and increasing inflation. A workman had to work a full day to earn his own food, for a denarius (v. 6) was a day's pay for a laborer, and a quart of wheat was a day's rations. To provide for his family, the workman had to buy barley, ordinarily fed to animals. Oil and wine were not affected, the implication being that famine was felt most by the poorer classes and least by those who used luxury items.

Millions of persons are starving today in foreign lands, and not a few in our own country. Many of them would be happy to eat the food Americans buy for their dogs and cats.

• *Death* (vv. 7, 8). The breaking of the fourth seal led to the appearance of the most fearsome of the four horsemen. Grim and fleshless, Death appeared riding an "ashen" horse—the greenish white color of putrifying human flesh. He was followed by Hades, the abode of the dead.

War naturally follows imperialism, or the spirit of conquest. Economic pressure and famine naturally follow war. Death is the logical consequence, and rides close behind the first three of the horsemen.

All four of these horsemen have been riding in every age of human history.

Today the population explosion seems to have taken men by surprise. At least they are not coping with it effectively as yet, with the result that the third and the fourth horsemen are galloping over vast areas of earth's surface. No doubt a further intensifying of these four woes will be seen in the future.

Why should these horsemen be treated, in this passage, as though they were appearing for the first time? Perhaps because this occasion is the first time they will be definitely linked with the final accomplishment of God's redemptive purpose. They are pictured in this passage as heralds of His judgment and agents of His retribution.

• *Martyred Dead* (vv. 9-11). After the fifth seal had been opened, John saw the souls of men and women "under the altar"—perhaps the altar of the heavenly temple (cf. 11:19). These were Christians who had died for their faith.

Martyrs are people who take their religion seriously. Most believers tend to be cautious in the extent to which they commit themselves and what they have to God, but martyrs stake their very lives on what they believe.

These martyrs were waiting. Apparently they were not completely happy, for they asked God to avenge their blood—not for the sake of the personal injustices they had suffered, but for the insolent contempt men had shown to the One for whose sake the martyrs had been slain.

God doesn't always rectify immediately the wrongs about which His people pray. He acknowledged the martyrs' just complaint and provided them with white robes, but counseled them to wait a little longer until others, who also must die for their faith, should join them.

How about you? Are you willing, as the martyrs were, to commit to God the injustices done you? Are you willing to wait patiently for God to settle the score, rather than lash out in retaliation?

• *Cosmic Disturbances* (vv. 12-17). The opening of the sixth seal produced a combination of cataclysmic cosmic disturbances unprecedented in human history. They remind us of what the Lord Jesus said about signs in the sky and about the powers of heaven being shaken. We can't imagine how the sky, which is not a solid object, could be split apart, or how the stars of heaven, which are suns hundreds of light years distant, could "fall." Undoubtedly the language here describes what *seems* to observers to take place. This is not a scientific account of God's judgments, but a graphic description from a human point of view.

We may be certain that these events will be terrifying to behold, and will grip the minds of earth dwellers with abysmal terror.

Man now knows enough about nuclear power and other elemental forces so that he could virtually destroy the earth. Should we think it strange that God, who created all things and who stored the atom with its unbelievable power, should be able to unleash wholesale destruction?

Overwhelmed by these catastrophic developments, men asked for the hills to fall on them. They did not so much want to get away from the physical disasters that were destroying them as to hide—if it were possible—from the presence of God and from the wrath of the Lamb (v. 16).

It is hard to realize that the same Jesus who pleads for admission into our hearts (Rev. 2:20) will one day unleash the dreadful judgment of an angry God. Today men despise the gentle Lamb who died to take away their sins, but in that day they will try at any cost to hide from Him. Only those who have been cleansed from their sins by His atoning blood will be able to stand.

The Two Multitudes (Rev. 7:1-17)

Revelation 7 is a sort of parenthesis in the chronicle of judgment. Here we read about two groups for whom God, in the time of judgment, made special provision.

First 144,000 Jews were sealed, or preserved. The identity of the tribes mentioned here has been lost today, but God could recover them. However, the numbers may be symbolic and deal with Israel as a national unit.

The unnumbered multitude (vv. 9-17) standing before the throne had come out of the Tribulation (v. 14). Some think they represent the Church, raptured before the Tribulation begins. Others identify them as a host of persons who come to believe on Christ after the Rapture.

This group represents those redeemed through personal commitment to the Lamb and removed from the experience of tribulation into the security and serenity of the throne room of God. Hunger and thirst, the heat of the sun, the bitterness of tears—these were now forever behind them. The Lamb Himself was to feed them, lead them to fountains of living water, and wipe the tears from their eyes.

Even today, though for a time your outward circumstances may remain unchanged, God is ready to satisfy your hungry heart, to shelter you during affliction, and to give you—in *any* condition, the comfort of His presence.

The Trumpet Shall Sound (Rev. 8:1-5)

When the seventh seal was opened, a hush of suspense fell over the heavenly scene, and seven angels appeared, ready to sound seven trumpets.

The seven seals represented general principles of judgment that have to a greater or lesser degree operated through the ages, but the trumpets, and the bowls that followed them, represented intensifying forms of judgment preliminary to our Lord's return.

6

Trumpets of Doom

Revelation 8:6—11:19

If you watch television, as most people unfortunately (?) do, you know how a station will show "previews" of programs to be telecast at some later time. Showing people provocative scenes in advance will arouse their interest and hopefully assure their watching the feature when it is aired.

The four chapters of The Revelation which we study this week cover a wide area of God's future judgments on earth and terminate with a "preview" of the grand climax toward which all creation moves—the time when our God and His Son will take over the kingdoms of this world and Christ will reign.

This glorious climax is preceded by the fearful judgments of God on man's sin. These judgments are described as happening in three series, or sequences, which are depicted as the seven seals, the seven trumpets, and the seven bowls. (The chart on page 6 may help you understand this arrangement.)

The opening of the seventh seal was the signal for the sounding of the seven trumpets, each of

45

which represented a judgment. This indicates that the trumpet judgments were all part of the seventh seal, and that they extend beyond the first six seals in time.

Tenney comments that probably the seven seals, the seven trumpets, and the seven bowls that follow the trumpets all conclude with the return of Christ. Some think the three sets of judgments are simultaneous. This may not be true, says Tenney, but it is quite likely that all of them end together. When the last bowl is poured out, a voice out of the temple of heaven announces, "It is done" (16:17).

From Worse to More So (Rev. 8:6–9:21)

For centuries God has waited for men to repent and turn to Him, but in the time symbolized by the events John describes in these chapters, the day of opportunity will end.

The first four trumpet blasts, like the opening of the first four seals, produced cataclysms in the world of nature:

• The sounding of the first trumpet (8:7) brought down on the earth a deluge of hail, fire, and blood. This cut crops to pieces, destroyed agricultural resources, and left the earth slimy and smelly. A third of earth's trees and grass was destroyed.

• The second trumpet blast (vv. 8, 9) was the signal for a huge body, "something like a great mountain," to fall into the sea. This could be a huge meteor similar to the one that left a vast crater in Siberia; another smaller one once fell in Arizona. The meteor John saw killed a third of all marine life and also wiped out a third of earth's shipping vessels.

• The third trumpet (vv. 10, 11) was the signal

for another falling body—a great "star." This could be another meteor. It fell upon earth's rivers, polluting supplies of fresh water and poisoning men who drank them. This catastrophe suggests atomic fallout, a phenomena with which our generation is all too familiar.

• At the blast of the fourth trumpet (vv. 12, 13), judgment fell on the heavens themselves, and earth's span of light and darkness was affected—a change that could be calamitous.

Like the first four seal judgments, the first four trumpet judgments seem to be a unit. They were followed by other visitations much more severe (cf. v. 13) and of a different nature.

• As John heard the fifth trumpet sound (9:1-12), he saw the supernatural world invade the world of men.

There was a great deal of speculation, a few years ago, about flying saucers and the possibility of an invasion of earth from outer space. The creatures in view in Revelation 9 were not from another planet. They originated from the bottomless pit and from the Euphrates River, where they had been imprisoned to await this hour. The "star" that came to release them may have been Satan himself.

There is a great gulf fixed between the world of men and the world of demons; otherwise Satanic influence would be even more common. The rise of witchcraft, astrology, and Satan worship today indicates that the barriers may be breaking down. In any case, the fifth trumpet will bring on a supernatural invasion of evil.

These demons, in the form of locusts, attacked not vegetation but men. Their weapon was a poisonous sting like that of a scorpion. An ordinary scorpion sting is seldom fatal, but it is one of the most painful experiences an insect can inflict on a human being. The venom sets the blood on fire, as it were, and the effect may last as long as several days.

The victims of these locusts suffered intolerable pain for five months. They tried to commit suicide to escape their agony, but were unable to die.

Some think these locusts symbolize some kind of mechanized warfare, but when we attempt symbolical interpretation of such passages as this we can find in the text almost any meaning we look for. It is therefore better to stick to a literal interpretation. There *is* a world of supernatural evil beings.

• The sounding of the sixth trumpet (vv. 13-21) led to another invasion of the human race by supernatural forces. Four evil spirits bound at the Euphrates River were released, and they brought up another army of supernatural beings—perhaps an order of demons.

It is not easy to explain how the Euphrates River figures in this judgment. Water, traditionally, is a barrier to evil spirits. The Euphrates, of course, is in the region of old Babylon—a region which Isaiah predicted would be occupied by demons after it had been desolated (Isa. 13:21, 22).

These four spirits commanded a great host of supernatural beings. Their horsemen killed a third of all living men. Their mounts breathed fire and smoke and had sting-like tails.

Most commentators take 9:15 to mean that this judgment will take place at the year, month, day, and hour of God's appointment. Others take it to mean that the affliction will last for 13 months (a year, a month, a day, and an hour), or until a third of all living men have been put to death.

It is extremely significant to notice that the men who survived the judgments of the fifth and sixth trumpets felt no inclination to turn to God in repentance for their sin and to ask Him for mercy. The human heart, as Jeremiah tells us, is "desperately sick." Men have no awareness, ordinarily, of their sinfulness.

Instead of repenting under affliction, men will continue in their beloved sins, a few of which are listed at the close of chapter 9:

Idolatry. Men today not only are allowing money, pleasure, and "freedom" to come between them and God, but are actually engaging, more and more, in the worship of Satan.

Murders. In the world of organized crime, human life is cheap. More and more wanton murders are being committed. In the days of the Tribulation the earth will be stained with the blood of crime's victims.

Immorality. Study the motion picture page in any metropolitan daily paper to see what kind of "entertainment" people want. Someone has said that the time in America is sex o'clock. Increasing immorality has heralded the downfall of more than one culture. Our own civilization may be an exception only because the Lord Himself will overthrow it at His coming.

Thefts. Most men today are materialists. They want the so-called good things of life, and they will stop at nothing to acquire them.

No More Delay (Rev. 10:1—11:14)

Much as there was a parenthesis, as it were, between the breaking of the sixth and the seventh seals, there was also an interlude after the sounding of the sixth trumpet.

The angel that John saw at this time closely resembled previous descriptions of the Lord Jesus (cf. 10:1; 1:7, 13-16), and may have been none other than He. Perhaps the little scroll in His hand was the scroll mentioned in chapter 5.

Seven peals of thunder spoke at the appearance of this angel, but John was forbidden to record the message of the thunder. There is more to God's purposes than He has revealed.

This angel announced God's final judgment. "There shall be delay no longer" (v. 6), he declared. The redemptive purpose of God in Christ (cf. Eph. 3:3-12) was to be brought to completion, and human history was about to be terminated.

The angel commanded John to eat the little scroll. It was sweet in his mouth but bitter after he had swallowed it. The Gospel may seem to be delightful, but the pronouncement of judgment, on which John was embarking, is a bitter responsibility.

John was then ordered to measure "the temple of God" (Rev. 11:1). This must have been the Temple on earth, rather than the one in heaven, because its outer courts were trampled by the Gentiles for 42 months (v. 2). The prediction may refer to the rebuilt edifice of which Ezekiel wrote. The 42 months, or three and a half years, during which the Temple is in Gentile hands, may refer to the latter part of the seven-year period of tribulation in view in 11:3-13.

The two witnesses (vv. 3-14) were another feature of the "interlude" following the sixth trumpet.

These witnesses are linked with Old Testament prophecy (v. 4; cf. Zech. 4:14). Their power to halt rainfall and turn waters to blood suggests they were Elijah and Moses. Both these men left earth under unusual circumstances; both appeared with Christ on the Mount of Transfiguration; and both are mentioned in the Old Testament prophecy of the Restoration (Mal. 4:1-6).

The two witnesses were invincible so long as their testimony was incomplete. Someone has observed that any Christian is immortal until his work for God on earth has been finished. These two men, who witnessed for God during the period of judgment, had power to kill their enemies with fire.

After the two witnesses had served God's purpose, their enemies put them to death and rejoiced with callous hilarity at overcoming them through the beast that came up out of the abyss, or pit. Their enemies were so depraved that they denied these two servants of God a decent burial, and their bodies lay in the street for three days, the objects of scorn and hatred.

The joy of the rabble, however, was short-lived, for the witnesses were resurrected before the eyes of their enemies and carried up into heaven. This miracle was followed with an earthquake so terrible that even the depraved men left on earth were filled with terror.

"And He Shall Reign" (Rev. 11:15-19)

The sounding of the fifth and the sixth trumpets introduced the first two or three "woes," or judgments of particular intensity. The last "woe" was heralded by the sounding of the seventh trumpet, after which John heard a mighty chorus of heavenly voices proclaiming, "The kingdom of the world has become the kingdom of our Lord and of His Christ; and He will reign forever and ever."

Even in heaven, this announcement demanded worship, and the 24 elders fell on their faces before Almighty God and adored Him, thanking Him because at long last, after infinite patience with rebellious, sinful, godless mankind, He had taken up His great power and begun to reign "forever and ever."

Now the time was at hand for judgment, for the vindication of the people of God who have been mistreated through the ages, and for the destruction of the wicked.

Now the temple in heaven was opened and the ark of the Covenant was revealed—an indication that a demonstration of divine power was to take place. There were flashes of lightning, peals of thunder, an earthquake, and a great hailstorm.

Doesn't your heart throb with excitement as you read? Don't you long for the day when our Christ will take up His power and reign?

7

The Winning Side

Revelation 12

A good many persons criticized the United States Government's handling of the war in Viet-Nam. They were far from enthusiastic about a "limited war" in which bombing planes, for example, were for months restricted in the damage they were allowed to impose upon the enemy.

Many people felt it would have been far better to hit the enemy hard and end the war as quickly and decisively as possible, thus cutting casualties to a minimum.

One national commentator, in his analysis of the war, declared that this conflict had taught us one thing: that if a nation gets into a war it had better fight to win.

God's people are actively involved, whether they like it or not, in the greatest war of all time. As we have already pointed out, it is the warfare between right and wrong. Our Lord and His angels head the forces of righteousness, and the devil, his demons, and his fallen angels are included in the hosts of wickedness.

Revelation 12 pictures this war as a conflict between a woman and her descendants on the one hand, and Satan and his hordes on the other. It shows us that this war extends even into heaven, and it reveals the secrets of victory. This makes the chapter important to you, for you want to be on the winning side in this age-old fight.

Halfway involvement is no more adequate in spiritual warfare than it is in physical fighting.

The Three Persons (Rev. 12:1-6)

Revelation 12 is a controversial chapter, and interpretations of it vary widely because it involves symbolic language.

The word "sign" (v. 1; "wonder," AV) is used in the Greek to let us know that in what follows the "sign" is a symbol for something else. On the highway, a sign marked "Danger" is not in itself perilous; it simply warns that something dangerous is ahead.

It is of course important that we interpret Bible types and symbols correctly. However, we are to exercise genuine Christian charity toward believers who disagree with us.

• *The Woman* (vv. 1, 2). John saw a woman clothed with the sun. She stood on the moon and wore a crown of 12 stars. She was pregnant and her child was just about to be born.

The Roman Catholic Church teaches that this woman was Mary, but in view of verses 13 and 14, this view seems unlikely. In another interpretation, the woman represented God's people of all ages—spiritual Israel.

A third view, favored by evangelical Christians,

holds that the woman was Israel. The 12 stars represent the 12 patriarchs. This interpretation ties in best with the symbolic meaning of the Child.

• *The Dragon* (vv. 3, 4). There is no doubt about who the dragon represented. The text plainly states that he was a symbol for Satan, the devil (v. 9). The dragon was fiery red, the color of blood and of war. His seven heads symbolized political authority; his ten horns represented absolute power. His tail indicated his influence, which he used as a weapon.

The stars mentioned here may have represented angels, as they do in Job 38:7. Revelation 12:4 would seem to indicate, in that case, that a third of the angels in heaven, influenced by Satan, may have joined him in a revolt against God which led to their being thrown from heaven to earth.

There is nothing in this passage to indicate the reason for Satan's downfall, but it may be linked with the sin of pride (Ez. 28:17).

All through the Old Testament, we can trace the devil's antagonism toward God's people. He made a definite attempt to defile or destroy the line of promise—the ancestral line of the Messiah—and so to frustrate the coming of the Redeemer into the world. God, however, prevented the Jews from being exterminated in Egypt and in Babylon, and in due time Christ was born.

Satan also made many attempts to keep our Lord from going to the Cross. He may have inspired Herod's slaughter of the children at Bethlehem, the storms on Galilee in which Jesus could have drowned, the Nazarenes' effort to push Him over the precipice, and the premature plots of the Jews to kill Him.

Satan is pictured here in a symbolic way, but don't make the mistake of thinking he is a mythological being. The whole Bible teaches plainly that evil is headed up by a definite person who is antagonistic toward God and His purposes and who is doing all he can to thwart the fulfillment of God's plans.

• *The Man-Child* (vv. 5, 6). As you have already seen, the Child which the woman was about to bring to birth was Christ. This is clear by a comparison of verse 5 with Psalm 2:7-9.

The fight between the woman's Seed and Satan began in the Garden of Eden, where God foretold (Gen. 3:15) how it would end.

Those who take the woman to symbolize God's people in every age believe the Man-Child to be a symbol not only of Christ but also of those who are faithful to Him and who will one day rule the nations with Him (v. 5; cf. 20:4).

The woman's flight into the wilderness (v. 6) is often taken to symbolize Israel's fleeing from Anti-Christ during the second half of the seven-year Great Tribulation, the period covered by the trumpet judgments and the preaching of the two witnesses. The woman's safety was assured, for God had prepared a place where she might hide out and "be nourished."

Thrown Out! (Rev. 12:7-12)

The conflict, mentioned above, between Satan and *his* angels and God and His angels is described in these verses.

Since first being thrown out of heaven, Satan has had access to the throne of God on occasion, and he has used that privilege to accuse God's people (v. 10). The word "devil," in fact, means "accuser."

The time will come, this part of John's vision indicates, when war in heaven will result in the total and permanent banishment of Satan and his hosts from heaven.

This will spell trouble on earth (v. 12). Because he will know that he has been defeated, and that he will shortly be confined to the bottomless pit, Satan will release a fierce storm of wrath against mankind. He will concentrate on God's people, particularly the Jews, and the last and most dreadful outbreak of anti-Semitism will result.

Persecuted but Protected (Rev. 12:13-17)

Foiled in his desire to destroy the Man-Child, the dragon turned his attention on the woman. Whatever else we read into the symbolism here, the woman certainly represents the nation Israel, here in the form of a remnant of Jews who will repent of their unbelief and turn to Christ as their Messiah.

The persecution Satan will unleash upon the Jews will be fearsome, but God will deliver them. He provided a means of transporting the woman to a place of refuge.

The dragon sent out a "flood" after the woman. This may represent military forces (cf. Jer. 46:7, 8), but perhaps an earthquake (Rev. 12:16) will swallow his troops.

Baffled again, the dragon turned his attention to "the remnant of the woman's seed" (v. 17)—perhaps Jewish Christians scattered here and there. For a time, these Hebrew believers will bear the brunt of Satan's hatred.

Three great truths emerge clearly from this difficult passage:

• Believers are helping the work of Satan when they join the forces of antisemitism. To hate the members of *any* minority group is to put oneself to that extent on the side of evil. Injustice, discrimination, and oppression have no place whatever in a believer's attitudes or actions.

• God can protect and deliver His people when it is in His will to do so. Christians have often been martyred, for it is not always God's will that His people escape death, but even in hopeless circumstances God is able to deliver them.

• Satan cannot forever frustrate God's purposes. In the end, God's will is going to be accomplished. Satan is powerful, but God is infinitely *more* powerful.

How to Win

Of special interest to you is the three-fold secret of victory in the warfare between good and evil (cf. v. 11):

• First, God's people overcome "by the blood of the Lamb." In dying for our sins, Christ redeemed us from Satan's power and made all God's blessings available to us.

This means that salvation is the first and essential step toward victory. Unless you have laid hold, through personal trust, on the forgiveness that may be yours through the redemptive power of Jesus' blood, you have no basis for expecting God to help you in the warfare with temptation and sin. And without God's help, victory will be utterly impossible.

• Second, victory comes through the Word to which God's people bear witness—through the Gospel, or Good News. It includes not only the announcement that eternal life is available to all who will receive it through faith, but the fact that victory, peace of mind and heart, and spiritual fruitfulness are available for those whose life is Christ. Most of us settle for far less than we could have.

• Third, the victors "loved not their lives to the death."

A woman in a Bible class, asked what she would do if she could choose between giving up her faith and giving up her life, replied. "Oh, I think it's our *duty* to save our lives! Don't you?"

The early Christians did not think so. They died rather than compromise in order to save themselves.

Maybe it sounds paradoxical to speak in the same breath of being a victor and of dying for one's faith. Many Christians act as the world does—as if death were the end of everything worthwhile. They "believe" in heaven, of course—but they are anxious to put off going there just as long as possible.

If you appraise life as God sees it, however, you will be willing to die gladly rather than extend your time on earth at the cost of loyalty to Christ. Such complete commitment to God assures your being an overcomer, regardless of whether or not you live on, here, to celebrate your victory!

8

Empire of Evil

Revelation 13 and 14

Suppose a man appeared on the international scene today who was able to convince the world that he could provide permanent peace, international prosperity, minimal taxes, and complete freedom from moral restraints.

In a culture that yearns for peace, is frankly materialistic, and is wantonly dedicated to the pursuit of pleasure, how do you think most people would react?

Isn't it rather obvious that such a man would be acclaimed quickly as a world ruler?

The Scripture foretells such a person. His name is Antichrist, but he is also called the Man of sin, the Son of perdition, and "the beast." He will weld the nations into one world, to be sure, but it will be a world given over to wickedness and utter rebellion against God. The present tendency to immorality and chaos will come to fulfillment and the worship of God will be outlawed.

Premillenarians and amillenarians alike agree that world conditions are going from bad to worse and that the only effective solution is the return of our Lord. The world of unbelievers, however, will accept the "solution" offered by Antichrist.

Here Now and Coming Too (Rev. 13)

Standing on the seashore in his vision, John saw a grotesque beast coming up out of the sea (vv. 1-3). He seems to have been a sort of composite of the four beasts which Daniel saw (Dan. 7:1-7), though of course the description of him is symbolic. The sea, in Scripture, often represents restless, storm-tossed humanity, which would indicate that the beast was a human being, perhaps a Gentile. His seven heads and ten horns indicated the fullness of the authority he received from the dragon, Satan (v. 2).

The man of sin, described in 2 Thessalonians 2, is apparently the same individual as this beast. We cannot be sure what "blasphemous names" (Rev. 13:1) means, but the designation was appropriate because the beast announced that he was God, and demanded worship (2 Thes. 2:4).

Perhaps the beast was the impersonation of a historical person, or had had a previous existence on earth, for he had been given a fatal wound but had recovered (Rev. 13:3).

The devil is a great imitator. He has his counterfeit of the Christian Gospel, his counterfeit miracles, and his counterfeit of Christ's resurrection. Here, too, is the counterfeit of the Christian Trinity. The dragon, Satan, is the counterfeit of God the Father. The first beast, Antichrist, is the counterfeit of God the Son. The second beast (vv. 11:18) is counterpart to the Holy Spirit.

"The whole earth" (v. 3) followed after the beast. This is the "one world" toward which civilization has been moving in recent decades. The world worshiped the beast and the dragon who supported him (v. 4). Only those whose names are written in the Lamb's book of life (v. 8) resisted him, and those who refused to venerate him were persecuted unmercifully. Their resistance ended in death (v. 10).

The ten horns of the beast deserve special attention. Many commentators link them with the ten toes of Daniel's image (Dan. 7:8), which they believe refer to a ten-kingdom revival of an empire resembling that of ancient Rome. Some see in the European Common Market a possible beginning of such a ten-kingdom power. Early in 1972 the number of nations in the Common Market reached ten—perhaps a significant event. It is widely reported that a diligent search is presently under way for a man to "head up" the market. His position would be a powerful one indeed.

The second beast which John saw arose out of the earth. The beast out of the sea is usually linked with military power; the creature that came out of the earth is taken to represent religious authority, and was called the false prophet.

This beast was different from the first. He had two horns like a lamb, which indicates that he too is an imitation of Christ and is religious by nature. (Remember that "religion" is by no means the same as "Christianity"!)

"In these two beasts," comments Tenney, "comes the final union of religion and the state. The religion exalts the state and the state supports the religion. The reign of Antichrist will be a totalitarian state that makes a cult, or religion, of evil."

The idea that the state is supreme, popular in the days of absolute monarchies, when the power of the state was vested in the ruler, has been emphasized by Communism. Josef Stalin, for example, during his lifetime had life-and-death control over more people than any other ruler. He held sway over a sixth of the globe—and did all he could to get the other five sixths under his control.

The trend toward the supremacy of the state is being carried forward, today, even by "democratic" governments like that of the United States. Our governmental bureaucracies are accumulating more and more power. The state's control over industry, commerce, and business gets stronger and stronger. Taxes have long since passed the upper limit regarded by economists as "safe." Governmental regulation gets more extensive and more complete.

The false prophet will induce men to make an image of Antichrist, and by some trickery or demonic power he will give life to this image and enable it to speak. Those who will not worship the beast or receive his mark will not be allowed to buy food or engage in business, and many of them will starve. Others will be martyred.

Such a situation is far from impossible today. Perhaps you can recall the days of World War 2, when gasoline and food were rationed and when these commodities could not be bought without the proper stamps issued by the government. In Russia, only loyal members of the Communist party were eligible for food stamps. A similar situation will come about in the days ahead.

No one can be sure what "666," the number of the beast, means. In Greek, the letters of the alphabet have numerical values and are used instead of figures. Perhaps the numerical values of the letters in Antichrist's name will add up to 666. Attempts have been made to link this figure with Nero, Hitler, Stalin, and other dictators. You may be sure that when Antichrist appears on the scene, God's people will have no difficulty establishing his identity.

The spirit of Antichrist has been abroad in the world since the first century (1 John 4:3). It is the spirit of Christ-denial and of resistance to and rebellion against God's Word. The reign of the beast will bring to a full and dreadful climax man's rejection of God and His truth.

Thinking and honorable men are shocked today by the corruption and extravagance in almost every government. Executive, legislative, and judicial officials at all levels are often working chiefly to keep themselves in office and to increase their salaries, rather than to serve the voters. Crime is rampant in both city and country, for criminals have learned that the adage, "Crime doesn't pay," is simply no longer true. Crime pays—and it pays very well—for a while. The number of criminals who serve time has been reckoned as low as two percent of the number of crimes reported, which means that a criminal has one chance in 50 of going to jail.

Add to the picture the sharp practices of business today, the tactics of labor leaders, the drug traffic, drunkenness, immorality and other sex crimes, and the staggering indifference of men toward the claims of God, and you will agree that we live in an evil world. But today's world conditions will be like a prayer meeting compared with the evil abroad in the world during the time of Antichrist.

Another Interlude (Rev. 14)

Chapter 14 is another of the parenthetic passages inserted into the action throughout The Revelation.

It opens with John's vision of the Lamb on "the Mount Zion" (lit.), surrounded by 144,000 persons. They do not bear the mark of the beast, but the mark of the Father (v. 1), and they may well be the same 144,000 whom John saw earlier (7:1-8) on earth. They had kept themselves from defilement—not always easy!—and had followed Christ regardless of the cost. Now they have been translated into heaven and rejoice with the Lord before the throne (v. 5).

The rewards of faithfulness are great!

The chapter closes with a series of announcements that link the balance of the book with the seventh trumpet and summarize events still future. They are like the announcements of victory a herald would make on the stage during a Greek drama. It would not be practical to fight the battle in front of the audience, so the herald would appear and simply state how the conflict had turned out.

• *The everlasting Gospel* (vv. 6, 7). An angel flew from heaven to announce "an eternal Gospel" —a command to fear, glorify, and worship God. By this time all mankind will be familiar with the Gospel, and there will be no need for the angel to go into details about its nature. His announcement will simply serve as a reminder to men.

• *Fall of Babylon* (v. 8). Another angel declared the fall of Babylon—an event more fully described in Revelation 17 and 18. This city's iniquities had polluted the entire earth.

• *Beast Followers* (vv. 9-13). A third angel announced the condemnation of those who had worshiped the beast or its image. Those who, during the reign of Antichrist, conform to the godless world system will share the fate of the beast and suffer with him forever. God made hell for the devil and his followers; the only reason human beings will be sent there is that they have not accepted God's salvation.

This vision was followed by another of the seven "beatitudes" of The Revelation: "Blessed are the dead who die in the Lord from now on . . . that they may rest from their labors, for their deeds follow with them" (v. 13). Unbelievers are destined for endless torment, but Christ's followers will enjoy unending rest. The deeds of unbelievers will be left behind them at death, no matter how talented. The deeds of Christians follow them. God's people can lay up an imperishable treasure in heaven.

• *Christ returning* (vv. 14-16). Next John saw the Son of man, seated on a white cloud of glory and holding a sharp sickle, ready to reap the sheaves. At the invitation of another angel, He garnered earth's ripened harvest.

• *Fruit gathered* (vv. 17-20). This vision was closely linked to the previous one. John saw still another angel come out of the heavenly sanctuary with a sickle in his hand to gather "the clusters from the vine of the earth." The angel gathered the vine and cast it into the winepress of the wrath of God.

Some think verse 20 refers to Armageddon, the last great battle before Christ's earthly reign. The fight will be a bloody one, and even if the language here is figurative, it speaks of a time of fearful vengeance when God will "trample out the vintage where the grapes of wrath are stored." The words remind us of how Isaiah saw the triumphant Redeemer coming back from the winepress (Isa. 63:1-3).

Three great truths emerge from these powerful chapters of Scripture:

1 Evil is in the ascendant today. Godly people are in a minority; those who hate the Gospel are getting more numerous, more popular, and more powerful. Things are going from bad to worse.

2 The overflow of the forces of evil will be total, as depicted in the angelic announcements of the judgments to be unfolded in the rest of The Revelation. Satan and his followers face complete defeat at the hands of God.

3 Righteous men—those who are trusting in the Lord Jesus Christ and whom God has justified because of their faith—will either be removed from the scene of carnage by the hand of God or protected through the judgments that will desolate the earth.

And if God can take care of His people in that awful day, He can—and will—take care of you *now*.

9

Judgment
and Judgment

Revelation 15 and 16

Ed Grantland, your neighbor, is an intelligent man who holds a good job as purchasing agent for a large mail-order house. He likes to discuss current events and world conditions, and you have had some interesting talks with him.

Theology—to put it mildly—is not Ed's strong point. His convictions about the future have not been shaped by Bible teaching.

"The history of the world," he says firmly, "is simply a sequence of causes and effects. Each event follows from a natural cause, and is itself a cause of future events. The future, then, depends entirely on how men handle the present. Whether we are heading for disaster or for Utopia is strictly up to us. No other philosophy of history is sound."

What do *you* think?

Is history a mere sequence of causes and effects? Does the future depend entirely on what men do?

Or is history, as someone has put it, "His story"? Is it the outworking of God's purpose to sum up, in Christ, all things in the heavens and upon the earth? (Eph. 1:10). And if so, what do we learn from The Revelation about the part that God's judgments have in bringing His purposes to pass?

Revelation 15 and 16 may shock you—especially if you think that because God is love He will never really act in shattering judgment on sin and sinners.

We usually associate God's glory with His grace, mercy, and other qualities that bring blessing, joy, and life into the experience of human beings. But God's glory will also be enhanced by other elements in His nature about which we may not often think. It will be revealed, for instance, when His holiness impels Him to crush utterly the forces of evil.

You have studied the judgments linked with the opening of the seven seals (6:1—8:5) and with the sounding of the seven trumpets (8:7—11:19). Now, in chapters 15 and 16, we come to a third series of judgments that are even more terrible than either of the first two. They are the pouring out on earth of the bowls of the wrath of God. This series of calamities brings God's judgment to a close.

No time is mentioned as to when these bowls are poured out, but it is logical to conclude that these judgments, like the others mentioned in the book, take place during the second half of the Tribulation, a period variously referred to as lasting 1,260 days, 42 months, or 3½ years. And the fact that men will still be suffering the effects of the first bowl when the fifth bowl is poured upon them (16:2, 11) leads some scholars to conclude that the bowl judgments will occur in rapid succession, perhaps near the end of the Tribulation.

Remember that the events recorded in The Revelation are not necessarily narrated in the order in which they take place. There is a certain amount of overlapping—we cannot be sure just how much. For instance, the collapse of Babylon has already been mentioned (14:8), but the details are not given until chapters 17 and 18. (The chart, p. 4, may be helpful.)

Bowls Filling Now (Rev. 15)

The word "sign" (v. 1; translated "wonder" in AV, 12:1, 3; 13:13) indicates that symbolic language is being used. Here the seven angels, with their plagues, represent the dreadful judgment of a God who cannot tolerate sin.

Before the throne of God John saw those who had overcome the beast praising God and the rightness of His judgments. They sang "The Song of Moses and of the Lamb," combining the redemptive themes of both the Old and the New Testaments. The Song of Moses was sung by the Israelites after God had overthrown the Egyptians in the Red Sea; the Lamb had fulfilled all that the Passover lamb of Moses prefigured.

Then the temple in heaven was opened (v. 5; cf. 11:19) and the seven angels came out. They were clothed in clean, bright linen, symbolic of holiness, and wore golden girdles, representing righteousness.

The four living creatures before the throne had previously called the four riders that symbolized conquest, war, famine, and death (4:6-8). Now one of the living ones gave the seven angels the bowls filled with the wrath of God—bowls which man's sin is undoubtedly filling today, and which must be almost full to capacity as men pursue their selfish ways, contemptuous of God and of His Word.

God is the One who lives forever and ever (v. 7).

Men in their abject folly think God is optional, or that if they reject Him he does not exist so far as *they* are concerned.

They couldn't be more wrong.

Fearful to Contemplate (Rev. 16)

John heard a great voice, probably the voice of God Himself, sending the seven angels out on their mission. As they emptied their bowls, the results were catastrophic. The white-hot coals of God's anger wreaked unimaginable havoc on the entire earth.

• *Sores* (v. 2). The first bowl produced a terrible plague of painful sores that afflicted the followers of Antichrist. This judgment resembled the plague of boils that came on Egypt just prior to the Exodus. Perhaps it was induced by corruption or by physical filth—but it is neither necessary nor even advisable for us to think we must find a "natural" explanation for each of the strange eschatological events predicted in the Bible. There is no good reason for not taking these descriptions literally.

• *Sea to Blood* (v. 3). The second bowl, when it was emptied, extended the results of the second trumpet judgment (8:8). The rest of the ocean turned to blood and all marine life came to an end.

• *Rivers to Blood* (vv. 4-7). The third bowl turned rivers and springs to blood, too, extending the effects of the third trumpet. The beast and his followers, who had shed the blood of God's people, were given blood to drink. This completed the vengeance for which the martyrs under the altar had called on God (6:9, 10), and now John heard the martyrs praise the Lord for His righteous judgments.

• *Sun Intensified* (vv. 8, 9). The contents of the fourth bowl strengthened the heat of the sun to such an extent that men were scorched by it. Perhaps protective elements in the atmosphere, which hold back some of the ultraviolet and infrared rays of the sun, will one day be temporarily removed. The results were painful in the extreme—but men, far from repenting of their sins, blasphemed God's name.

• *Darkness* (vv. 10, 11). The fifth bowl plunged the entire earth into darkness. Imagine this condition. Men were gnawing their tongues for pain because of their sores. The intense heat would produce insatiable thirst, but the earth's water supplies had been turned to blood. The darkness of midnight would have a profound effect on morale.

Guides in Mammoth Cave, Kentucky, sometimes seat their groups of visitors and then turn out all the lights, leaving tourists in a darkness more black than any midnight. Some visitors talk volubly, some stifle a scream, and all grow tense. Imagine what would happen if such a state of affairs were worldwide—and particularly if other calamities had made artificial light unavailable.

Again we read that men did not repent (v. 11) of their sins. Instead, they hardened their hearts against God. Perhaps they said, "If there were a God, would He do *this* to us?"

• *Euphrates Dried Up* (vv. 12-16). The sixth bowl was emptied on the Euphrates River, which also figured largely in the sixth trumpet judgment (9:13, 14). This time, however, the river was dried up to prepare the way for the kings of the East.

The Euphrates, in Scripture and geographically, has always been the barrier between the East and the West. The barrier out of the way, the armed forces of "the kings of the east" will find it easy to march against the western world. With more than 600 million people in China, 400 million in India, and countless millions more in other neighboring areas, the Far East will be a formidable foe.

The economic and military combinations of the last days are beyond the scope of this study, but other Scriptures imply that the rulers of the east will fight on the side of Russia and the Arab nations against Israel. No doubt this coalition will be brought about, humanly speaking, by international agreements. Behind the power politics involved, however, will be "spirits of demons" (vv. 13, 14)—Satanic influences which will impel human rulers to unite for an attack on God's people.

Earth's last great battle will be fought on a Palestinian plain extending inland from the Mediterranean between Samaria and Galilee, where the town of Megiddo is located. Here is Har-Megiddo, or Armageddon, "the hill of Megiddo." This prospective battlefield has on several occasions been red with blood. It was here that Barak defeated the Canaanites (Jud. 4:15) and Gideon dispersed the Midianites (chap. 7).

• *Natural Disturbances* (vv. 17-21). The final bowl was poured "into the air," and John heard a voice—probably that of God Himself—announcing, "It is done!" (cf. 11:1-5)

Once again there were earthquakes—but this time they dwarfed all similar disturbances of recorded history. Jerusalem was divided into three parts, the great cities of the world tumbled into ruins, and the map of the earth was changed as islands vanished and mountains disappeared. The judgment climaxed with a tremendous fall of gigantic hailstones, weighing from 50 to 150 pounds each.

All these changes will pave the way for a new start, during our Lord's reign, for this purged and restored and redeemed earth.

God's purpose is that this earth become the scene of the kingdom of His Son, the Lord Jesus Christ. Unregenerate men, including most of the holders of high political positions in this nation and in others, have no knowledge of—and no desire for—this goal. They are working out their own purposes, usually selfish and often wicked. But God is using what they do, and overruling their motives, to bring His own aims to pass.

Judgment will put away forever the enemies of God. It will cleanse the earth of the defilement it has suffered at man's hands. It will pave the way for God's new creation, in which righteousness, peace, and blessing will abound.

10

Civilization Falls Flat

Revelation 17 and 18

Without any warning, during the height of the evening rush hour on December 16, 1967, the bridge over the Ohio River at Point Pleasant, West Virginia, collapsed. Cars, trucks, and people were hurled into the icy waters beneath, and 20 persons lost their lives.

The bridge had been standing for many years, and the public took its reliability for granted. Engineers who plan and build bridges calculate stresses and strains carefully and always allow a wide margin of safety. Bridge failures are therefore rare. Like most disasters, they are always unexpected.

Thinking people today, in view of the rising might of communism, the inherent weaknesses of democracy, the great increases in immorality and crime, and the ecological (environmental) crisis, are beginning to wonder whether or not our present culture can survive. But the vast majority of people, in spite of all the warning signals, are confident that our civilization will continue indefinitely. The fact that no civilization of the past has ever lasted indefinitely does not seem to figure in their thinking. John Average Citizen has an imperturbable confidence in the *status quo*.

The Bible, however, has a good deal to say about the course of human history. It tells us plainly that it is God's plan to destroy our civilization and to replace it with something infinitely better.

God's program is not one of gradual improvement of this earth. Man's efforts are not going to "bring in the Kingdom." The City of God is not being planned or built by men; it will come down out of heaven.

Revelation 17 and 18 give us a dramatic picture of the eventual destruction of the world system in which we live. It is represented, or symbolized, in this passage, by both a woman (chap. 17) and a city (chap. 18). Chapter 17 shows us our culture as God sees it; chapter 18 shows it to us as man sees it.

As God Sees Us (Rev. 17)

The third literary division of The Revelation, introduced by the phrase "in the Spirit" (cf. 1:10 and 4:2), extends from 17:1 to 21:9. This vision has to do with the completion of God's work of reclaiming the earth. The final division (21:10–22:21) describes heaven and tells us the terms of admission to its glories.

One of the seven angels who had taken part in the bowl judgments (17:1) took John to a wilderness and showed him the judgment of "the great harlot who sits on many waters."

This woman was dressed in clothing that suggested wealth and self-indulgence. She was devoted to immorality, which often symbolizes, in the Bible, compromise with evil. She held a cup of wickedness with which she had corrupted both the rulers and the common people of earth. She sat on a monstrous beast, which must have been Antichrist (cf. v. 3; 13:2). This beast "was, and is not, and yet is" (v. 8, AV), which may indicate that Antichrist will have had a previous earthly existence and will be brought back to life. He will rise up out of the abyss (cf. 13:1) and, after receiving the worship of those who do not belong to God, will be cast into perdition. This description has led some to think Antichrist may be a reincarnation of Judas Iscariot—a rather fanciful notion.

John was not left to wonder who the woman was. On her forehead was the name, "Babylon the Great, the mother of harlots and of the abominations of the earth" (17:5).

Babylon, in Scripture, is a "bad" name. In earliest times, rebellious men built the tower of Babel there and God destroyed it. The city was later the capital of the great Babylonian Empire, and was known for its cruelty, lust, and rapacity. God overthrew it, using the armies of Medo-Persia as His tools.

The seven heads of the beast on which the woman rode are called mountains, and a mountain, in Scripture, often symbolizes an empire or kingdom (as in Isa. 2:2). This view is supported by the mention of seven kings (Rev. 17:10). A series of kingdoms may be in view here—the one under which John lived (the Roman Empire), five earlier kingdoms (Egypt, Assyria, Babylonia, Medo-Persia, and Greece), and one kingdom that in John's day was still future. Many Bible scholars believe that this seventh great world power will be made up of ten subsidiary political units, each with its own ruler (v. 12). These ten kings will derive their power from Antichrist and will share his rule (v. 13), finally fighting with him against Christ (v. 14).

Various interpretations have been offered for the woman, Babylon. Scholars think she represents a system of culture and religion that will be supported by Antichrist, and some Protestant scholars have linked her with the Roman Catholic Church. But why not point to certain segments of Protestantism which have slipped in apostasy and corruption and have in some instances completely abandoned faith in the Christ of the Bible?

It is much more likely that the great harlot symbolizes an apostate world church that will dominate the religious, economic, and political scene. Political rulers supported the woman for the sake of the benefits she was able to give them, but when she had served her purpose they burned her with fire (v. 16). God controls men's actions even when they deny His existence, and it is He who inspired the rebellion that led to the harlot's destruction (v. 17).

The "waters" under the harlot (17:1, 15) are the peoples, multitudes, tongues, and nations on which she is seated. "She is," observes Tenney, "supported by the peoples, as well as by the empires, of the world. This breadth of expression means that she cannot be identified with any *one* movement. She is the religious and aesthetic aspect of godless civilization, which has debased faith into superstition, worship into idolatry, devotion into mad frenzy, and deity into demonism."

As Men See Their World (Rev. 18)

God sees the world's pleasures as tawdry, its

wealth as trash, its pretensions as cheap. Men see Babylon quite differently. They prize the very things that in God's sight are worthless or even dangerous.

Revelation 17 closes with the statement that the harlot was "the great city which reigns over the kings of the earth" (17:18). And in chapter 18 Babylon is described not as a woman but as a world metropolis.

Scholars disagree as to whether or not the Babylon in view here is a literal city. Isaiah predicted the total destruction of ancient Babylon and declared the place would never again be inhabited (Isa. 13:19, 20). To this day, the site is a wilderness. Desert nomads are said to believe it is haunted by evil spirits.

Some scholars, however, point to the phrase "the Day of the Lord" in Isaiah's prophecy, and think it indicates that the prophet was speaking about a *future* destruction of a Babylon yet to be rebuilt. "Babylon," then, may, symbolize some future world capital, a center of godless culture that will embody all the abominations represented by the harlot—a great world center of religion, commerce, and what men call "the good life."

Babylon, of course, *may* be a term applied figuratively to some present world capital of this present world system—London, Paris, or New York. Or, it may represent the sum of all the godless elements in our civilization. These chapters may well have both literal and spiritual applications.

The kings of the earth, though they destroyed Babylon (16:17), will lament her passing, perhaps because of the pleasures they enjoyed there. They will join the "merchants" (18:9-19) in mourning the disappearance of the business and the luxuries for which Babylon was so famous. The people of the last days, it seems, will be preoccupied with "gracious living"—with luxury and self-indulgence. You have no doubt noticed this trend among Christians!

Babylon's passing dealt a paralyzing blow to commerce and involved many traders in financial ruin (18:17). Commerce and trade are indispensable to the present state of affairs; there is nothing wrong with them until men make a financial profit the chief goal of their lives.

The destruction of Babylon will mark the end of man's vaunted civilization. The "finer things" of life —for instance, music (v. 22a)—will be swept away in her overthrow, along with more materialistic pursuits ("craftsmen," v. 22b) and activities that provide the basic needs of life ("millstones," v. 22c).

Even the homely scenes of quiet family life (v. 23) will become things of the past. Babylon's Very Important People will have used their influence to pollute mankind in order to gain riches for themselves (v. 23), and this is their punishment.

How about the leaders of *our* industry and commerce and finance? How about our manufacturers and distributors? Will they escape the same condemnation?

In the midst of all the wailing and lamentation, however, there will be rejoicing—in the heavens (v. 20).

It seems harsh to rejoice over the fall of even an enemy, but because Babylon has always been the foe of God's people, and because she has had no sympathy with truth, no faith in God's message, and no interest in His goals, heaven will rejoice at her downthrow.

God warns His people to "come out" (v. 4) of Babylon. Steer clear of the lust of the flesh, and the lust of the eyes, and the pride of life (1 John 2:15, 16)!

No matter how comfortable you are in Babylon, nor how prosperous or popular, God expects you to flee for your life from the wrath to come. No one can find permanent happiness or true joy in Babylon—in the world. The world system is passing away, and only those who obey God will remain.

Our culture is doomed. For all its appeal to our appetites and our intellect, it is—in God's sight, rotten. If you look at it as God sees it, you will not find it hard to keep yourself from being unduly involved in what passes today for "good living." The wit and wisdom of unsaved men, the world's culture and pageantry, will have no appeal whatever for you if you look at them from the perspective of God's Word.

11

Total Victory

Revelation 19:1—21:8

People are more interested in eschatology—in "last things"—today than they have been in many years. Complete these sentences to check on your EQ—your eschatology quotient. Correct your answers as you study, and give yourself 20 points for each correct sentence:

1 The white horse that will come from heaven after the destruction of Babylon will be ridden by . . . and followed by. . . .

2 The weapon by which Christ will defeat His enemies is. . . .

3 The marriage supper of the Lamb is for . . . but the supper of the great God is for. . . .

4 Satan will be confined in the . . . for . . . years.

5 The wicked dead will be judged from the record of their . . . and from the absence of their names from the. . . .

Antichrist, Satan's great counterfeit of the Lord Jesus, our Saviour, first appears in Revelation 13. In chapters 17 and 18 we have read a symbolical description of the economic and social order over which this fearsome being will rule, and learned how it is completely destroyed during God's judgments on earth. In chapters 19 and 20 we now read about his military and political downfall and about the other events that give our Lord final and total victory over the forces of evil.

For the Birds (Rev. 19:1-21)

John had heard a great lamentation among the political rulers and commercial tycoons of earth when Babylon, the great city symbolizing the wealth, culture, economics, politics, and religion of the last days, was symbolically destroyed as an angel threw a great millstone into the sea (18:21). The catastrophe seemed to rob the lives of earth-dwellers of all meaning, interest, and joy.

Not so, however, with the hosts of heaven! John heard around him, there, a great multitude join in a thunderous anthem of praise and adoration, the words of which inspired Handel's magnificent *Hallelujah Chorus*. Even Handel's sublime music, however, was no doubt vastly surpassed by the majestic strains which the apostle heard as he stood there before the glorious throne of Almighty God. The 24 elders, the four living creatures, and all the hosts of the redeemed joined together in magnifying the Lord God Almighty (vv. 2-6).

"Let us be glad and rejoice," the mighty chorus sang, "for the marriage of the Lamb has come, and His bride has made herself ready!" (v. 7). The Church, of course—the corporate body of all the redeemed of the whole Christian era—is Christ's bride (Eph. 5:23-27, 32). She wears the white robes of righteousness which He provides (Matt. 22:11), and the time has come when she and her Lord will be forever united. The intimate relationship between Christ and believers is not always apparent today, but at last it will be clear to all (cf. Col. 3:3, 4).

Does the glory of that coming moment encourage you when you tend to be downhearted or discouraged? It ought to! As marriage should be one of the greatest occasions in human life, so being a participant in the marriage of the Lamb will be an experience of unimaginable blessedness and everlasting joy.

Then the vision of the marriage supper dissolved and John looked at another sight of vastly different character. He saw the Lord Jesus Christ astride a white horse, going forth at the head of the armies of heaven to complete the conquest of earth. Our Lord's majestic power and sovereignty were symbolized by the crowns which He wore. His flaming eyes pictured His omniscience—that nothing is hidden from His knowledge. Don't be puzzled by the fact that His sword came from His mouth (v. 15; cf. 1:16); this simply means that He will not use military power or strategy in winning earth's last battle. He will simply speak the word and His enemies will be overcome by total defeat. His word of power, which brought the universe into existence, will completely vanquish Satan and his hosts.

John heard an angel inviting the birds of the air to the supper of the great God, to eat the flesh of those, great and small, who were to suffer defeat (Rev. 19:17, 18).

The battle was over almost before it began. Antichrist and his false prophet were cast alive into the lake of fire, and his followers perished misera-bly. The birds gorged themselves on the flesh of the fallen.

What a contrast between the marriage supper of the Lamb and the great supper of God!

God's patience is tremendous. He is so long-suf-fering that men make the mistake of thinking His patience is inexhaustible. But when God begins to act in final judgment, nothing will stand before Him.

What about the lake of fire? Is it a literal place? If so, where is it?

Surely the universe is large enough so that some-where on its outer fringes there can be a place where God will finally dispose of those who have persistently flouted His goodness and rejected His salvation.

The lake of fire does not involve extinction of existence. After a thousand years there, the beast and the false prophet were still alive (20:10).

Millennium—and Rebellion (Rev. 20)

There are three chief views on the Millennium, the thousand-year reign of Christ on earth:

• *Postmillenarians* believe the Church will suc-ceed in making the world better and better. After a state of perfection (or near-perfection) has lasted for about a thousand years, Christ will return to judge the earth and raise the dead, after which the eternal state, heaven, will commence. There are not many postmillenarians today, for almost everyone is painfully aware that the world just *isn't* getting bet-ter and better.

• *Amillenarians* think the thousand years are figurative and may refer to the reign of Christ and the resurrected saints in the spiritual world. They also believe Christ will return to judge the living and the dead, but do not believe a thousand-year period, during which He reigns on earth, intervenes between His coming and final judgment.

• *Premillenarians* take Revelation 20 literally. The Scripture plainly states that, after the overthrow of Antichrist, Satan is chained in the abyss for a thousand years, and that during this period the resurrected followers of Christ reign with Him for that length of time.

Those who do not take the Millennium literally sometimes believe that God's Old Testament promises to the Jews have been transferred to the Church because of Israel's failure to accept her Messiah. Most premillenarians, however, believe the promises of future Jewish national greatness will be literally fulfilled during the thousand years.

Think of it! For ten centuries, the devil's influence will be missing from the world scene. The survivors of the tribulation period will be ruled by Christ and His saints, with every advantage that good government, a high order of scientific knowledge, and the best educational facilities can give them. That will be earth's golden day, when even nature and the animal kingdom will be affected. Read such passages as Isaiah 11, 35, and 60, and Psalm 72, for glowing descriptions of what the redeemed earth will be like after the renewing, restoring hand of God has removed the curse of sin.

As Tenney points out, the thousand years will be no "vacation" for the saints. The ruined earth, devastated by the judgments it has undergone, must be rehabilitated, and it's very likely that God will give man a hand in the process.

One would think that after a thousand years of righteousness, peace, and prosperity, mankind would be completely won over to the Lord Jesus Christ, whose reign will be the means of bringing about such ideal conditions.

Not so!

The human heart is incurably wicked, and what happens at the close of the Millennium is proof conclusive that no amount of good external influence can change the corrupt nature of men. No amount of education, no high standards of living, no exposure to righteousness, can take the sin out of human nature. Only when men are transformed by a personal encounter with Christ—only when they become partakers of the divine nature by putting their trust in God's Son, the Saviour, do they become new creations (2 Cor. 5:17).

That is why, at the end of the thousand years, when Satan is released from his dungeon, he will find it easy to deceive men and to round up an innumerable multitude (v. 8) to make an attack on Christ and the holy city.

There will be "no contest," however. Fire will fall from heaven and consume the hosts of wickedness. After this skirmish, Satan will join Antichrist and the false prophet in the lake of fire, where he will spend eternity.

The world's history ended with what happened next. John saw a great white throne—white being emblematic of holiness and purity—and One sitting on it from whose face heaven and earth fled away in an attempt to escape the penetrating perceptiveness of deity.

Then the dead, small and great, came from the

grave. They came from the sea and from hades, the place of departed spirits where went the rich man who wanted Lazarus to cool his tongue with a drop of water. They came to the great white throne, to stand in fearsome, dread expectancy before the One against whose grace they had sinned.

John saw this multitude judged from two books. One was the indelible record of their works (vv. 12, 13). They will learn, at last, that "good deeds" and "religion" are no substitutes for personal trust in Christ. And because their names are not written in the Lamb's book of life—the register of those who are trusting Christ—they will be condemned. In the terrible anguish of hopelessness—utter and final hopelessness—they will be cast into the lake of fire, prepared for the devil and his angels, because they refused the grace of a loving God.

City of God (Rev. 21:1-8)

As the vision of grim judgment faded from his view, John saw yet one more vision—a vision that was entirely glorious.

Heaven and earth had passed away, and there was no more sea. John saw a new heaven and a new earth. Perhaps the first earth had been purified in some way (2 Peter 3:7)—we cannot be sure about all the details of the awesome events in which history will culminate. At any rate, John saw the holy city, new Jerusalem, coming out of heaven from God, made ready as a bride adorned for her husband (v. 2). He heard a great voice announce from heaven that God would dwell with His people and be their God. The eternal state, the new order for society, heaven, was ushered in. The long-awaited rule of permanent righteousness was about to begin.

John was seeing a preview of the most stupendous event in all the history of man.

In the description of heaven given in the opening verses of Revelation 21 is a tender promise—God will wipe away all tears from the eyes of His people. There will be no more death nor sorrow, no crying nor pain. The former things—the hard things, the unpleasant things, the wrong things—will all have passed away. God's people will say good-bye forever to heartache, discouragement, disappointment, and frustration. They will come at last into the full joy of the great salvation in which, down here, hope plays such a prominent part.

Who has not longed for a "land of beginning again"—a place where one can start over, leaving behind him his mistakes and failures? In heaven, God will make all things new. What a day that will be!

You need not wait until then, however, to be a victor with Christ. You can be sure, today, that you are on the winning side. Stop trying to be good enough to get to heaven, admit to God that you can't meet His requirements, and accept the righteousness He offers freely to all who depend on Christ instead of on their own efforts.

Settle it right now!

12

Heaven
on Earth

Revelation 21:9—22:21

"You paint a pretty picture of heaven," an unbeliever said to his Christian neighbor. "But just suppose that after you die you find that what you believe about the future life is not true. What then?"

"Well," answered the Christian good-naturedly, "I find life with Christ a wonderful adventure. I couldn't possibly be any happier, here and now, with any other convictions. If it should turn out that I've been mistaken about heaven, I won't be any the worse off after I die. But if what I believe is *true*, where will *you* be after you die?"

Heaven is no cunningly devised fable. The Lord Jesus Christ and His followers are neither wicked liars nor gullible fools. The Saviour gave His personal promise that He was going to prepare a place for His people (John 14:2). That place is the subject of this chapter.

In John's previous vision, one of the seven angels with the bowls transported him to a wilderness (17:1) and showed him a vision of the great harlot, who was also described (chap. 18) as a city, the capital and center of the world's trade, culture, and religion.

Another City (Rev. 21:9—22:5)

In John's next and last vision, one of the seven angels took him to a great and high mountain (21:10) from which he could get a better view of another city, the city of God, the new Jerusalem, which he had previously seen (v. 2) coming down from heaven to earth.

The first city John had seen was a harlot; she was seated on a beast bearing the names of blasphemy. The second city was a bride, the wife of the Lamb. The first city was defiled and evil and godless. The second was radiant and pure and altogether glorious.

The description of this city is a glowing one, but language lacks words to picture it adequately, and John therefore had to resort to symbols, as he did in describing the glorified Christ (chap. 1).

The city came from heaven and from God, and it shone with the glory of God; it resembled a great precious gem (v. 11). God is light, and He has frequently manifested Himself in the form of light—especially in the Shekinah, the brilliant glory that went before the Israelites in the wilderness and that filled the holy of holies in the Tabernacle and in the Temple. Because of the brightness of God's presence, the New Jerusalem had need of neither sunlight (v. 21) nor artificial illumination (v. 21). God's presence will do away with sin, ignorance, and evil, all of which are symbolized by darkness.

Like practically all the cities of John's time, this

city had "a great and high wall," some 215 feet high (v. 17)—three times the height of an ordinary city wall. Such a wall would suggest, to John's first readers, absolute security from all danger. The believer's security may be a controversial issue today, but there will be no room for dispute about the safety of those who find themselves within the walls of the City of God!

Though the city was walled, there were gates on all four sides, suggesting ready access. The city will not be all there is of heaven, for the earth, in its renewed form, will also be in use. The nations of the redeemed, and their rulers, will bring into the city their glory and honor (vv. 24-26). This may be a reference to trade, learning, or scientific achievement. Whatever is worthwhile and noble and good will be brought to the city to glorify the Lamb, the King of kings.

Since the city "comes down to earth from heaven," people have speculated about its geopraphical location on earth. Where will it be deposited? Such speculation is futile and unnecessary. The oceans may have disappeared (v. 1) and the contours of the land will doubtless have been radically altered by the Tribulation judgments (16:20). There will be adequate space for the city!

A city, however, is more than buildings and streets. The important element of a city is people. The jeweled foundations of this city bore the names of the 12 apostles and the pearly gates carried the names of the 12 tribes. This may well indicate that heaven is for all men of all ages—of Old Testament times and New Testament days—who have called in faith on the name of our great and loving God.

John saw the angel measure the city—an indication of its substance and reality. Its breadth and length and height were equal—about 1,580 miles each way, or the distance from Chicago to Miami.

Whether or not the dimensions of the city are to be understood literally is a matter of dispute. It is hard to imagine a city in the form of a solid cube. And how could a city as high as it was wide have a wall? Or, was the city built up on pyramid style, with a series of stages or decks? (A modern architect has drawn plans for such a self-contained city, but on an infinitely smaller scale.)

These details are of little importance; the important truth is that this city, unlike most of our modern metropoli, did not "just grow." It was planned, and its Architect was God. Men will not build it by their work and effort—it already exists, and at the proper time God will place it upon the redeemed earth.

Robert Ripley, who for years ran a column called "Believe It or Not," once pointed out that all the people who have lived since Adam's day would be terribly crowded in a city 1,580 miles square. But Mr. Ripley overlooked three facts: the fact that the city will be as high as it is wide and long; the fact that not all heaven's inhabitants will necessarily be inside the city at the same time (for heaven will include the renewed earth); and, finally, the fact that by no means all the people who have lived since Adam's time are going to need space in heaven. New Jerusalem will be only for those who have put their trust in God and have been forgiven on the basis of the death of the Lord Jesus Christ. The holy city is only for the people of God.

There was no temple in the city (v. 22). The presence of God and of the Lamb will pervade the place, making a special place of worship unnecessary. And of course the complete absence of sin made atoning sacrifices unnecessary, too.

The throne of God was the focal point of the city, and from it proceeded the river of the water of life (22:1), suggesting that God is and forever will be the source of supply for all man's deepest needs.

The person of the Lord Jesus is not described in detail in this final chapter of The Revelation, but it is significant that He is repeatedly mentioned here as the Lamb, a title which speaks of His sacrifice for the sin of the world. Only those who honor Him now as their Saviour will be able to serve and worship Him then as their King, who will share the throne with the Father (5:6).

The prophetic portion of The Revelation ends at 22:5 with the assurance that God's people will reign eternally with Him. "They shall see His face, and His name shall be on their foreheads" (v. 4). This symbolizes not only that He possesses them and that they are safe in Him, but that they are in possession of the divine nature forever.

This purpose of God having come to fulfillment, no further predictive word is needed.

Postscript (Rev. 22:6-21)

The remainder of the book is in the nature of an epilogue which shows us clearly that The Revelation has been given us with a practical purpose in view.

Here are the last two beatitudes of the Bible: they promise blessedness to those who heed the words of the prophecy (v. 7) and to those who "wash their robes" and qualify to have a share in the city of God (v. 14). This is a clear reference to accepting the righteousness which God freely credits to those who put their trust in Christ as their Saviour.

Here, too, is the Lord's great promise, "Behold, I am coming quickly" (vv. 7, 20). Nearly 2,000 years have elapsed since those words were spoken, but a thousand years are in God's sight like a mere day (cf. 2 Peter 3:8). The idea here is more *imminence* than *haste*. His coming is possible at any time.

Here, too, is the advice that this prophecy, unlike that of Daniel, is not to be "sealed up" (Rev. 22:10, cf. Dan 12:0), because "the time is near."

The Lord's return has always reminded Christians of the judgment seat of Christ, when God's people will receive rewards for their service. This outlook implies that *action* is advisable. If believers are to earn rewards, *now* is the time for them to be busy. Time is flying and life is uncertain. Get busy for God today!

It is desperately hard to break habits that have become firmly rooted (v. 11). The overall tendency of an individual at the time of death will never be reversed. Those who are "filthy" in their sins will become more and more so during eternity; those who die "righteous" because of their faith in Christ will go on, in heaven, to new glories of holiness.

The Bible's last invitation goes out to all mankind: "Let the one who is thirsty come; let the one who wishes take the water of life without cost" (v. 17). Eternal life, salvation, is *for all who want it.* It is available freely—as a gift. The only qualification is that you must be willing to accept it on God's terms—not as something you earn or deserve, but as something you receive by putting your trust in the crucified Lamb of God, the Lord Jesus Christ.

The Bible's last warning is that no one presume to add to or take away from the words of this prophecy. From earliest times there have been men who have tampered with the Word of God in an effort to further their own personal interests.

Finally, the Bible's last prayer is found in 22:20: "Come, Lord Jesus."

God's greatest blessings for His people and for this earth are inextricably linked with the coming again of His Son. His return is our blessed hope (Titus 2:13), for when He appears we shall be like Him—we shall receive the fullness of our salvation, our glorified bodies, and we shall be with Him forever.

Can you join in this prayer? Or is Christ's coming a matter of indifference to you? Or is it something you'd rather not think about?

Take the water of life freely! Trust in the Lamb who died for you! And then be jubilant in the prospect of His coming again!